AF530491

FISCAL DEFICIT OF STATES IN INDIA

Edited by

JANAK RAJ GUPTA

ATLANTIC PUBLISHERS AND DISTRIBUTORS

Published by
ATLANTIC PUBLISHERS AND DISTRIBUTORS
B-2, Vishal Enclave, Opp. Rajouri Garden, New Delhi-27
Phones : 5413460, 5429987

Sales Office
4215/1, Ansari Road, Darya Ganj, New Delhi-110 002
Phones : 3273880, 3285873, 3280451
Fax : 91-11-3285873
e-mail : info@atlanticbooks.com
web : www.atlanticbooks.com

© The Editor, 2001

ISBN 81-269-0004-0

No part of this book may be reproduced in any form without permission from the publisher except for the quotation of brief passages in criticism

Typeset at
APD Computer Graphics, Delhi

Printed in India at
Nice Printing Press, Delhi

PREFACE

The growing fiscal deficit has been bothering both the Union Government and the State Governments. But over since the fiscal crisis of 1991, the concern about fiscal deficit has gained momentum. It is commonly understood that fiscal deficit implies excess of government spending over government receipts. But what it actually connotes has been vividly explained in the book. How this Western concept of defining a deficit budget has been thrust upon us? What are the limitations of concept of fiscal deficit? What are the implications of growing fiscal deficit? These are some of the questions which have been dealt with in this book. However, the greatest merit of the book lies in explaining the various concepts of defining a deficit budget. Each concept of deficit has its own logic and analytical use. Depending upon the policy perspective for sound fiscal management and the stage of the economy each concept of budget deficit has its own relevance and limitations. It is only when one properly understands the various concepts of deficit that one can interpret the implications of the various issues involved and thus offer useful suggestions for the sound management of State finances.

The book has been conceived as a prelude to solving the problem of growing fiscal deficit in the States as well as in the Centre. Though the problem of State finances in India was not very acute up to late seventies/early eighties, yet in the recent past the problem has deteriorated to an alarming proportion and until and unless a serious attempt is made to remedy the imbalances in the resource position of different States, the growing fiscal deficit will have serious social, political and economic implications. Therefore, considering the importance of the subject matter, the Editor wrote to the experts working in various Universities in the area of Public Finance with the request to contribute a paper covering the various facets of finances of their or any other State. The response received was very good and I am naturally beholden to all of them. It is only because of their active contribution that I have succeeded in presenting at one place the fiscal scenario of many States in the country.

This is a comprehensive book on the sound management of public finances. As a theoretical prelude, it is an important book for the students of Pubic Finance since it contains conceptualisation of the deficit budget. The book is also important for the policy makers and the academicians because it tries to identify the factors which have led to the present state of impasse on fiscal front and thereby offers useful policy prescriptions, both in the short-run and in the long-run, for sustainable size of public expenditure.

This book could not have seen the light of the day without the unstinted support and sacrifice of my wife Bimla who, in spite of my increased responsibilities, bore the entire brunt of household affairs.

JANAK RAJ GUPTA

CONTENTS

1

CONCEPTUALISATION OF FISCAL DEFICIT

—J.R.Gupta

To designate the deficit budget of the Government the usage of the term fiscal deficit has become very common. Before the concept of fiscal deficit was evolved, we have been talking about revenue deficit *i.e.,* deficit on revenue account, capital deficit *i.e.,* deficit on capital account, budget deficit *i.e.,* overall deficit, monetized deficit, deficit financing, etc. To understand the genesis of fiscal deficit, we shall have to first analyse its anatomy or components.

In fact the term fiscal deficit in the budget documents of the Government of India was perhaps first used in 1991, by the then Finance Minister, Dr. Manmohan Singh. Before him we have been talking about budgetary deficits and deficit financing. But deficit financing has been defined differently in the Western sense and in the Indian sense. And a proper interpretation of the usage of the term deficit financing in the two senses would enable us to understand the concept of fiscal deficit.

In the Western sense deficit financing denotes the technique of financing a deliberately created gap between public revenue and public expenditure, the method of financing resorted to is being borrowing of a type which results in a net addition to aggregate expenditure. However, in the Indian sense we have been defining deficit financing in terms of the overall budgetary deficit which means the aggregate of the deficit on both the revenue account and capital account. The First Five Year Plan has stated that :

The term 'deficit financing' is used to denote the direct addition to gross national expenditure through budget deficits, whether the deficits are on revenue account or an capital account. The essence of such a policy lies, therefore, in Government spending in excess of the revenue it receives in the shape of taxes, earnings of State enterprises, loans from the public deposits and funds and other miscellaneous sources. The Government may cover the deficit either by running down its accumulated balances or by borrowing from the banking system (mainly from the Central bank of the country and thus "creating" money).[1]

The Government may cover this deficits by : (a) running down its accumulated cash balances, (b) borrowings from the Central Bank and (c) creating new money.

Thus, in advanced countries deficit financing mostly takes the form of additional credit creation through the banking system. Hence, borrowing by Government either results in the activisation of idle deposits held in banks or by the private individuals themselves or in the creation of deposits by banks which purchase Government securities or bonds. Therefore, in the Western sense deficits budget means excess of expenditure over current revenue, *i.e.,* market borrowing do not constitute part of Government revenue, whereas in the Indian sense market borrowings are considered part of Government receipts.

From the above discussion it is clear that the concept of budgetary deficit may involve different technicalities which may give rise to different interpretations, though in a layman language it implies excess of public expenditure over public revenue. The few concepts of 'deficit' which are currently in vogue are discussed below :

Revenue Deficit or Deficit on Revenue Account

The traditional budgeting is divided into two accounts, *viz.*, revenue account and capital account. Revenue account implies the current revenue or revenue on current account. It includes the usual receipts of the Government from tax and non-tax sources. While tax receipts are obvious, non-tax sources include the usual administrative revenue, commercial revenue from public enterprises including revenue from social and economic services, fees including court fees, fines, etc. which the Government usually receives in a particular year.

Expenditure on revenue account or current account is the component of Government expenditure which it has to incur for purchasing goods and services for consumption purposes in a particular year. That is why sometimes this expenditure is also called consumption expenditure. The main components of revenue account expenditure are salaries including pensions, interest payments and subsidies. In fact the concept of revenue account might become clearer when we define capital account. Revenue deficit implies excess of revenue account expenditure over revenue account receipts. Since expenditure on interest payments is considered to be due to the past action of the Government, therefore, revenue account deficit net of interest payments is sometimes termed as *primary revenue deficit.*

Capital Deficit or Deficit on Capital Account

In India the main source of capital account receipts has been public borrowings which were resorted to by the Government in the past to build capital assets. In developing countries like India, where the Government has to play a crucial role to build economic and social infrastructure, the Government may have to generate enough surpluses on its own for investible purposes. It goes to the credit of the Government of India that in spite of wide spread poverty it has been generating more revenue than expenditure on revenue account up to 1970's. And these surpluses *i.e.,* excess of receipts over expenditure on revenue account were being transferred to capital account to be used for building capital assets. But the Government resort to borrowings since it cannot finance its entire expenditure on capital account, which includes expenditure on (a) gross fixed capital formation *i.e.*, building and construction as well as machinery and equipment, (b) increase in inventories including store and stock of foodgrains, (c) repayment of public debt and (d) capital transfers *i.e.,* grants for capital formation to the States, Union Territories or the Local Governments, gratuity and commuted value of pensions and other capital transfers. Therefore, borrowings are the major source of revenue on capital account. The other sources of revenue on capital account may be selling of assets or what we call now is disinvestment of public sector enterprises.

To understand the distinction between expenditure on revenue account and capital account, it would be better if these expenditures are defined in terms of the quantum of assets and liabilities created during a particular period. Receipts which increase the Government liabilities (like public borrowings) or reduce the public assets (like receipts from disinvestment of public sector expenditures) should be termed as receipts on capital account. Conversely any public expenditure which increases the public assets like expenditure on investment, renewals, repairs increase in inventories, etc. or reduces the public liabilities (like repayment of public debt and payment of commuted value of pension and gratuity) should be termed as expenditure on capital account. All other usual types of expenditure and receipts should be termed as those on revenue account. For example, take the case of payment of pension. The payment of regular pension is like payment of regular salary. Therefore, this expenditure is termed as expenditure on revenue account. But the payment of commuted value of pension, which reduces the liabilities of Government is treated as expenditure on capital account. It should be born in mind that because of its nature capital account has to be deficit, which is no harm.

Budget Deficit

The total budget is defined as the sum total of revenue account budget and capital account budget. Obviously total budgetary receipts would include receipts both on revenue account as well as those on capital account. And total budgetary expenditure would mean the sum total of expenditure on both revenue account and capital account. In this context before 1991, we have been talking about total budgetary deficit, which was financed by drawing down of previous balances, borrowings from the Reserve Bank of India, printing of new money, etc. These moves always led to net addition in money supply/money expenditure in the economy and was termed as deficit financing. Obviously, deficit financing was always inflationary that is why it was mostly dreaded.

Fiscal Deficit

Fiscal deficit is the difference between total receipts (excluding net borrowings) and total expenditure. In other words borrowings are not considered as part of Government receipts. As already stated, in the beginning this is what deficit financing means in the Western sense. For example, as per Keynsian prescription to fight great depression Government should create the deficit budget which may be either financed through the creation of new money or through borrowings of idle funds which were lying idle with the people and which need to be activated.

> The Government's income is from taxation; any expenditure in excess of tax receipts must be financed by borrowings or newly created money.[2]

Obviously deficit financing defined in the Indian context and in the Western sense carried different economic connotations having different economic implications. For example, deficit financing defined in the Western sense has to be less inflationary.

Coming specifically to the concept of fiscal deficit reduction of which carries the hallmark of every sound budget. As already stated broadly it denotes the difference between total receipts (net of borrowings) and total expenditure. That is part of the budget which is financed through public borrowings is termed as fiscal deficit.

> Gross fiscal deficit is defined as the difference between revenue receipts (net) plus non-debt capital receipts and the total expenditure including loans net of repayments. This is a measure, which captures the entire shortfall in the non-debt resources for financing the Central Government operations.[3]

To some commentators, however, "fiscal deficit is defined as the difference between total government expenditure (current and capital) and revenue receipts. It may be decomposed into debt-financed deficit and money-financed deficit depending on whether it is met by borrowing from the public or Reserve Bank of India."[4] Thus, if we deduct monetized deficit from the fiscal deficit, this may show debt-financed deficit. This view is useful for monitoring the growth of public debt which may lead to a situation of debt-trap after a certain limit. The recent decision of the Government of India (GOI) to introduce the Fiscal

Responsibility and Budget Management Bill, 2000, which seeks to put a cap on Government borrowing is a step in the right direction.

To reduce the fiscal deficit the two sides, *i.e.,* receipts and expenditure, must match. Now let us see what the Government is doing. Coming to the management of public expenditure first. Total expenditure has two sides : revenue account expenditure and capital account expenditure. As already said expenditure on revenue account comprises mainly of salaries (nearly 60-70 per cent), interest payments (30 per cent) and subsidies. Interest payments on public debt, because of past commitment can not be curtailed. So far the Government has failed to downsize, therefore, the axe has to fall on subsidies. One must have come across the often repeated rhetoric of the Government while presenting every budget that it would slash the quantum of subsidies so as to get hold over ever burgeoning fiscal deficit. But alas this measure has its own political compulsions and the result is ever increasing swelling of fiscal deficit. Thus, revenue account expenditure being broadly committed and of non-plan nature is very difficult to curtail.

Coming to the second component of public expenditure *i.e.,* expenditure on capital account. It is the major casualty. The public expenditure on capital account has been witnessing a downward trend. Not only public expenditure on economic infrastructure, *viz.,* power, transport, communication, etc., is being slashed even social infrastructure like education and public health are getting step motherly attention of the Government. While the former is being handed over to the private sector, the neglect of the latter has been causing a great social and economic tensions.[5] In fact when one examines the trends in public expenditure of the State Governments one would find that the States have found an easy way to cut capital expenditure and plan expenditure since they have no control over non-plan expenditure, which is of committed nature.

Now coming to the receipts side of fiscal deficit, which include tax and non-tax sources as well as receipts from disinvestment of public sector enterprises. Tax revenue of the Central Government as proportion to GDP has fallen from 8.0 per cent to 7.0 per cent, while non-tax revenue like fees and fines is mainly realized by the State Governments. Now what the Central Government is doing and even Finance Ministers are admitting that in order to reduce the fiscal deficit, they are showing an increasing proceeds from disinvestment of public sector enterprises. It is another thing that these proceeds are not being materialized. Now the point to debate is that proceeds from disinvestment are receipts on capital account because these proceeds directly lead to the depletion of Government assets. Therefore, a simple logic demands that these capital account receipts should be used for capital account expenditure *i.e.,* either for retiring the public debt or for reinvestment in remaining public sector enterprises. However, presently the Government has been using these receipts to meet the needs of current expenditure so that fiscal deficit is contained. The critics have rightly termed this as a 'Myopic Approach' to managing fiscal deficit. In the process we are eating our own assets. The main sufferers would be the future generations. The Government which is a custodian of the interest of future generations appears to have become callous to their interest.

Insofar as the other receipts are concerned *i.e.,* tax and non-tax receipts, which are broadly receipts on revenue account, these have their own economic logic. In India, already the tax rates have been quite high (though there is a scope to widen the tax-net) and in view of the globalisation, privatisation and liberalization these have to be further slashed, therefore, the Government will have to look towards non-tax sources.

Primary Deficit

Primary deficit which is defined as revenue deficit minus interest payments is usually termed as the main culprit of fiscal mismanagement. Interest payments are said to be due to the past action of the Government and hence unavoidable. But other items of expenditure are due to the current action of the Government and are, therefore, controllable to some extent. However, it may be emphasised that interest receipts are also due to the past contract of the Government. Therefore, the correct definition of the primary deficit should be :

Primary Deficit=Fiscal Deficit–Interest Payment+Interest Receipts.

But as shown in Table, which has been reproduced from the Reserve Bank of India Bulletins, primary deficit does not take into account interest receipts. Therefore, primary deficit figures as shown by the Government are underestimates to some extent.

Net Fiscal Deficit and Net Primary Deficit

Sometimes, for analytical use a distinction is made between gross fiscal deficit and net fiscal deficit, and gross primary deficit and net primary deficit. While fiscal deficit, defined as above, could be termed as gross fiscal deficit, net fiscal deficit may be defined as fiscal deficit net of 'loans and advances,' mentioned in capital account of the budget. That is 'loans and advances' are considered to be creating net assets of the Government and are not meant for consumption purposes. By the same logic one can say that other expenditure on capital account which is meant for the creation of capital assets should also be taken into account. If that is done, it will again bring us close to the earlier classification of deficit budget *i.e.,* deficit on revenue account and deficit an capital account. Similarly one can work out the net primary deficit by subtracting 'Loans and Advances' from the primary deficit.

Monetized Deficit

To finance the deficit budget, the Central Government, apart from other measures, borrows from the Reserve Bank of India which directly adds to money supply. This is due to the fact that borrowing from the Reserve Bank of India by the Central Government are simply book entries against which the latter can make the necessary payments.

Thus, monetized deficit is the increase in net Reserve Bank of India credit to the Central Government which is the sum total of net increase in the holdings of treasury bills of the Reserve Bank of India and its contribution to the market borrowings of the Government. But it should be remembered here that the monetized deficit, defined as above, may not be a perfect index to measure the inflationary pressure of the Central budget, because loans from the general banking sector also add to the liquidity and hence to the inflationary pressure of the economy. Similarly overdrafts to the States have also similar inflationary tendencies to generate.

Structural Deficit

The Eleventh Finance Commission considers that the structural deficit is the main bane of fiscal mismanagement. It is defined as a product of "the discretionary policy actions of an expansionary fiscal stance of the Government."[6] Obviously, structural deficit is expected to persist when the Government resorts to competitive populism resulting to needless subsidies without commensurate efforts to raise the required resources. Rising interest rates on public borrowings in the eighties was another structural factor contributing to fiscal imbalance. This has led to unsustainable growth of public expenditure. On the revenue side also virtual stagnation in the level of non-tax revenues and falling buoyancies of gross tax revenue from 1.15 during the eighties to 0.91 during the nineties in case of the Centre, and from 1.12 to 1.04 in case of the States would provide valuable insight into the character of the balances in the public finances in India.[7] It brings out clearly that deficits at both levels of the Governments are mainly structural. Until and unless corrective long term measures are undertaken, structural deficit is expected to persist. According to the XI FC, structural deficit registered "an increase during the 1980's accounting for more than 100 per cent of the FD of the Centre in the late eighties. Following the reforms initiated in the wake of the balance of payments crisis of 1991, the structural deficit went down, yet accounted for over 80 per cent of the FD. Structural factors were found to be dominant in the case of States also."[8]

From the above discussion it is clear that one can define the term of 'deficit' in a number of ways. Each definition or concept of deficit has its own logic and analytical use. Depending upon the policy perspective for sound fiscal management and the stage of the economy each concept has its own relevance and limitations.

REFERENCES

1. Government of India, Planning Commission, *The First Five Year Plan*, New Delhi, 1952, pp. 59-60.
2. Chick, Victoria (1983), *Macro Economics After Keynes, A Reconsideration of General Theory*, Heritage Publishers, New Delhi, p. 319.
3. G.O.I., Ministry of Finance, *Economic Survey* 1998-99, Aklank Publications, New Delhi, p. 23.
4. Mody, R.J. : On Defining the Fiscal Deficit, *Economic and Political Weekly*, Vol. XXVI, No. 38, Sept. 21, 1991, pp. 2223-24.
5. In fact the usage of the term fiscal deficit and the drive towards privatisation appear to the two sides of the same coin.
6. G.O.I., Ministry of Finance, *Report of Eleventh Finance Commission*, Aklank Publications, New Delhi, p. 10.
7. *Ibid.*
8. *Ibid.*

TABLE

Budget at a Glance

(Rs. in Crore)

Items	1996-97 (Accounts)	1997-98 (Accounts)	1998-99 (Revised Estimates)	1999-2000 (Budget Estimates)
1. Revenue Receipts (i+ii)	126,279	133,901	157,665	182,840
(i) Tax revenue (net to Centre)	93,701	95,672	109,537	132,365
(ii) Non-tax revenue of which :	32,578	38,229	48,128	50,475
Interest Receipts	22,106	25,323	30,544	33,034
2. Capital Receipts[@] of which :	74,728	98,167	124,247	101,042
(i) Market Borrowings	26,356	32,499	64,911*	57,461*
(ii) Recoveries of Loans	7,540	8,318	11,504	11,087
(iii) Disinvestment of equity in PSUs	455	912	9,000	10,000
(iv) Issues of Bonus shares	—	—	6	—
3. Total Receipts (1+2)	201,007	232,068	281,912	283,882
4. Revenue Expenditure (i+ii)	158,933	180,350	218,139	236,987
(i) Non-Plan	127,298	145,176	176,691	190,331
(ii) Plan	31,635	35,174	41,448	46,656
5. Capital Expenditure (i+ii)	42,074	51,718	63,773	46,895$
(i) Non-Plan	20,175	27,815	36,850	16,551$
(ii) Plan	21,899	23,903	26,923	30,344

Items	1996-97 (Accounts)	1997-98 (Accounts)	1998-99 (Revised Estimates)	1999-2000 (Budget Estimates)
6. Total Non-Plan expenditure (4i+5i) of which :	147,473	172,991	213,541	206,882$
(i) Interest Payments	59,478	65,637	77,248	88,000
(ii) Defence	29,505	35,278	41,200	45,693
(iii) Subsidies	16,125	19,487	24,683	23,838
7. Total Plan Expenditure (4ii+5ii)	53,534	59,077	68,371	77,000
8. Total Expenditure (6+7=4+5)	201,007	232,068	281,912	283,882$
9. Revenue Deficit (4-1)	32,654	46,449	60,474	54,147
10. Gross Fiscal Deficit [8-(1+2ii+2iii+2iv)]	66,733	88,937	103,737	79,955
11. Gross Primary Deficit (10-6i)	7,255	23,300	26,489	-8,045
12. Net Fiscal Deficit	46,394	63,062	70,988	68,547
13. Net Primary Deficit	9,022	22,748	24,284	13,581
14. Monetised Deficit #	1,934	12,914	16,750$$	N.A.

@ Capital Receipts are net of payments.

* Includes market loans, Zero Coupon Bonds, loans in conversion of maturing Treasury Bills, 364 day Treasury Bills, etc.

As per RBI records.

(-) Indicates surplus.

N.A. Not available.

$ With effect from 1.4.1999, a new system of transferring 75% of the net small savings collections to States and UTs from the public account is being introduced. With this change, the non-plan capital expenditure of the Centre during 1999-2000 is estimated to be lower by Rs. 25,000 crores.

$$ Upto March 1999.

Source : *Reserve Bank of India Bulletins*, October 1998 and April 1999.

2

DETERIORATING STATE FINANCES : NEED FOR RESOURCE MOBILISATION*

—P.K. Bhargava

The fiscal situation of the Centre as also of the States has been worsening over recent years. The quantum of fiscal deficit and revenue deficit has a tendency to increase at both the levels. The situation is likely to deteriorate further in view of the implementation of the recommendations of the Fifth Pay Commission. *The Economic Survey* 1998-99 in this context points out that :

> One of the factors which has strained the fiscal position of the Central Government has been the sharp escalation in its salary bill (pay and allowances) and pension payments... salary bill and pension payments now absorb more than one fifth of the total revenue receipts of the Central Governments.... (page 23).

The survey further emphasises that :

> The implementation of the Fifth Central Pay Commission recommendations at the Centre also provided a benchmark for pay revisions at the State level. This has led to a substantial increase in their salary and pension outgo thereby adversely affecting the fiscal health (page 23).

It may be pointed out here that the expenditure on salaries and pension of the Central Government employees has increased from Rs. 19,195 crores in 1995-96 to Rs. 33,840 crores in 1998-99 (Budget).

---

* This Article has been taken from the Mainsream, February 26, 2000. In this context the consent of Prof. Bhargava is greatefully acknowledged.

Some of the States — such as Punjab, Haryana, Tamil Nadu, Rajasthan, Madhya Pradesh and Uttar Pradesh — have also announced their decision to revise the salaries and wages of their employees. In view of the prevailing situation in the country, it is almost certain that all the State Governments, sooner or later, will have to revise the wages of their employees irrespective of the fiscal health of the respective States. According to one estimate, if the salaries of the employees of the State Governments, State financial and aided educational institutions are revised to the level of Central Government employees, the expenditure of the State Governments will increase by Rs. 20,000 — Rs. 30,000 crores a year. It only means that in the absence of adequate resources and with the existing fiscal strength of the States, the public finances of the State Governments will not only worsen but are likely to deteriorate so much that the situation may get out of control. It would, therefore, be prudent on the part of the State Governments to take certain remedial measures to avoid such a fiscal hazard.

Table 1 shows some of the disquieting features of the finances of the State Governments during the period 1990-91 to 1998-99 (Budget). The Table shows that during this period the total expenditure of the State Governments became almost three times but the expenditure on revenue account has risen faster. Further, the receipts on revenue account have not kept pace with the increase in expenditure on revenue account and that from the year 1994-95, the situation has tended to be somewhat alarming in view of the rapid increase in expenditure on revenue account.

In other words, the receipts on revenue account have lagged much behind the expenditure on revenue account and thus the State Governments have been faced to resort to increased borrowings from the Union Government as also from the market and other sources. This is reflected in the increasing interest bill of the State Governments. Table 1 shows that the interest bill of the State Governments during the period 1990-91 to 1998-99 (Budget) became more than four times (from Rs. 8654.8 crores to Rs. 36,399.3 crores) and that the increase has been significant from the year 1995-96. It may also be noted that interest payments constituted 12.1 per cent of the expenditure on revenue account in the year 1990-91 and that his percentage gradually increased to stand at 15.9 in 1998-99 (Budget). In 1996-97, this percentage in case of some of the poorer States — such as Bihar (17.2 per cent), Orissa (21.1 per cent), Rajasthan (18.9 per cent) and Uttar Pradesh (21.1 per cent) — was reported to be higher. If one looks at the interest payments as a percentage of the States' receipts on revenue account, the situation is somewhat more gloomy. It is clear from the Table that interest payments gradually increased from 13 per cent of the States' receipts on revenue account in 1990-91 to 17.9 per cent in 1998-99.

Another disquieting feature of the States' finances witnessed during recent years is the increasing expenditure on administrative services. This expenditure is further bound to increase in view of the revision of pay and allowances of the employees that has already been announced by some of the States and is likely to be followed, sooner or later, by other State Governments. Table 1 shows that expenditure on administrative services became slightly more than four and a half times (from Rs. 7018.4 crores to Rs. 37,786.1 crores) during the period 1990-91 to 1998-99 (Budget). As against this, the revenue receipts of the State Governments during this period were slightly more than three and a half (from Rs. 66,466.8 crores and to Rs. 203,176.0 crores). The Table also shows that the expenditure on revenue account in 1990-91 increased to 13.9 per cent in 1998-99 (Budget). It may also be noted that expenditure on administrative services constituted 10.6 per cent and 15.6 per cent, respectively, of the States' receipts on revenue account during the said years.[1] It is, therefore, a foregone conclusion that during the years ahead the expenditure of the State Governments on administrative services will increase rapidly and have its impact on their finances accordingly.

It is also clear from table 1 that the State Governments are significantly dependent on the Centre. The Table shows that the States' share in Central taxes and grants from the Centre increased from Rs. 26,884.8 crores to Rs. 75,110.7 crores in the period 1990-91 to 1998-99 (Budget) — 2.8 times. Thus, at present, almost one-third of the States' expenditure on revenue account is financed out of the transfers that are effected to the States from

TABLE 1

Selected Financial Indicators of State Governments

(Rs. in Crores)

Sr. No.	Item	1990-91	1991-92	1992-93	1993-94	1994-95	1995-96	1996-97	1997-98 (Revised)	1998-99 (Budget)
1.	Total Expenditure	91088.1	107929.4	119334.6	134648.5	161553.8	177583.7	202768.8	239712.9	273762.9
2.	Expenditure on Revenue Account	71775.8	86186.4	96205.2	109376.2	128439.9	145003.9	168949.9	196719.1	228810.8
3.	Interest Payment	8654.8	10944.4	13210.1	15800.5	19413.3	21932.1	25576.4	31235.4	36399.3
4.	Administrative Services	7018.4	7762.4	9344.4	10472.6	11664.3	13392.2	14853.3	17734.7	31786.1
5.	Receipts on Revenue Account	66466.8	80535.7	91091.1	105563.7	122283.7	136803.4	152836.4	177083.6	203176.0
6.	Share in Central Taxes and Grants from the Centre	26884.8	32073.6	38338.9	43570.8	44889.1	50043.4	58192.3	67791.4	75110.7
7.	3 as % of 2	12.1	12.7	13.7	14.5	15.1	15.1	15.1	15.9	15.9
8.	3 as % of 5	13.0	13.6	14.5	15.0	15.9	16.0	16.7	17.6	17.9
9.	4 as % of 2	9.8	9.0	9.7	9.6	9.1	9.2	8.8	9.0	13.9
10.	4 as % of 5	10.6	9.6	10.3	9.9	9.5	9.8	9.7	10.0	15.6
11.	6 as % of 2	37.5	37.2	39.9	39.8	34.9	34.5	34.4	34.5	32.8

the Centre in the form of the State's share in Central taxes and grants from the Centre. However, it may be noted that in view of the deteriorating fiscal situation of the Centre, there will be some kind of constraint on the Centre in providing assistance to the States on an increasing scale to bail them out of their deteriorating fiscal situation. This is going to be a serious problem of fiscal federalism in India. It would thus be prudent and obligatory on the part of the State Governments to make efforts to mobilise additional resources and/or avoid wasteful public expenditure.

Table 2 shows the increasing quantum of gross fiscal deficit as also of revenue deficit of the State Governments during the period 1990-91 to 1998-99 (Budget), excepting the year 1993-94. During this period, the quantum of fiscal deficit became slightly more than three times (from Rs. 18,787.0 crores to Rs. 59,276.6 crores) but the quantum of revenue deficit was slightly less than five times (from Rs. 5309.0 crores to Rs. 25,634.8 crores) during this period. The rapid increase in the revenue deficit of the State Governments is indicative of the fact that day-to-day financial requirements of the State Governments have far exceeded their day-to-day income. Thus, if the State Governments cannot reduce their day-to-day expenditure requirement, they have to necessarily

TABLE 2

Fiscal Deficit and Revenue Deficit of State Governments

(Rs. in Crores)

Years	Gross Fiscal Deficit	Revenue Deficit
1990-91	18787.0(3.5)	5309.0(1.0)
1991-92	18900.1(3.1)	5650.7(0.9)
1992-93	20891.2(3.0)	5114.1(0.7)
1993-94	20596.0(2.5)	3812.5(0.5)
1994-95	27696.8(2.9)	6156.2(0.6)
1995-96	31425.8(2.9)	8200.5(0.7)
1996-97	37444.4(2.9)	16113.5(1.3)
1997-98 (Revised)	51048.9(3.6)	19635.5(1.4)
1998-99 (Budget)	59276.6(3.6)	25634.8(1.6)

Note : Figures in brackets indicate percentage to GDP.

make efforts to mobilise additional resources and at the same time also avoid wasteful expenditure, wherever possible.

As a measure of reform in their tax structure, the State Governments have to think very seriously regarding mobilisation of resources, at least, from the relatively richer section of the rural population. Taxes on land and agricultural income have witnessed a rapid decline in their contribution in the States' tax system. However, the matter should be discussed at the National Development Council to evolve a consensus so that at least the relatively rich farmers may be taxed.

The relatively backward States like Bihar and Uttar Pradesh have a potential to raise their tax revenue by tightening the tax administration machinery. At present, the tax-SDP ratios vary significantly amongst States from about five per cent to 14 per cent. The matter requires a detailed scrutiny so as to mobilise additional resources.

During the recent period of reforms, the State Governments have been competing with each other in providing incentives/tax concessions to attract investors. For instance, Madhya Pradesh and Uttar Pradesh have adopted the most expensive open-ended sales tax exemption scheme which is likely to have an adverse impact on revenue and also cause unintended effects on resource allocation. It would, therefore, be in the fitness of things that the State Governments should not enter into a 'tax-war' to attract new investments; rather they should develop such infrastructural facilities which help to sustain development and at the same time provide an incentive for investment in the State.

The State Governments should take steps to withdraw gradually from all loss-making public sector undertakings. From the point of view of investment, any expenditure on them is self-defeating. In this context, for instance, it may be pointed out that till March 1997 the Government of Uttar Pradesh had invested Rs. 2680 crores in 49 public sector undertakings and that the accumulated deficit of these undertakings had reached Rs. 2758 crores thereby eroding the entire investment.

The State Governments have been incurring substantial losses on their electricity schemes, irrigation works and road transport facility. The beneficiary of these facilities ought to pay at least the user charges so that these schemes may be run on no-profit no-loss basis. It is reported that the gross subsidy to agriculture on account of subsidized power and irrigation alone works out to over two per cent of the national income. There is a considerable scope to rationalize and reduce these subsidies without adversely affecting the genuine interests of the farm sector. Further, many of the high-cost social sector services, such as higher education and specialized health services which are highly subsidized, need a careful scrutiny. The rationalization of user charges, at least in case of those who can afford to pay, will ensure efficient utilization of resources and improved service to the society.

It may also be pointed out that economy in expenditure is as good as generating additional resources. Hence, each State Government must address itself and identify the areas where the economy in expenditure can be practiced. This is a default task but in the context of the present resource inadequacy there is hardly any choice in the matter.

The above are some of the areas which need to be carefully scrutinized from the point of view of additional resource mobilization by the State Governments. Any laxity on the part of the State Governments in this direction will have serious repercussions on their finances. Hence, it would be in the fitness of things that the Eleventh Finance Commission in its scheme of evolving the principles and criteria for vertical and horizontal devolution of resources from the Centre to the States should introduce some kind of an appropriate performance criteria, in terms of additional resource mobilization, to be fulfilled by the States to make them eligible for Central devolution.

NOTE

1. It may be noted that interest payments constituted as much as 21 per cent of the States' own receipts on revenue account in 1990-91. This percentage increased to 25 in 1995-96 and further to 28 in 1998-99 (Budget). Similarly, the expenditure on administrative services as a percentage of the States' own receipts increased from 17 per cent in 1990-91 to 24 per cent in 1998-99 (Budget).

3

REVENUE MOBILISATION IN ORISSA STATE : AN INADEQUATE EFFORT*

—*Partap Ranjan Jena*

The Constitution of India has made elaborate provisions for both the States and the Union, relating to the distribution of taxes and non-taxes and power of borrowing. The arrangement of distribution of financial resources, is generally perceived to be not equitable due to the imbalances between revenue raising powers and expenditure responsibilities. Most of the buoyant sources of revenue, such as customs duty, corporation tax, etc., are in the purview of Central Government for the stated reason of administrative efficiency and the implicit desire to make the Centre strong *vis-a-vis* the States. This has culminated in Central Government having a comparative advantage over the States in raising revenues. But the fiscal responsibilities in meeting huge expenditures remained with the State Governments. Even the Central transfers in the form of grants and shares in Central taxes could not entirely put a lid on the growing deficits of State budgets, as is evidenced prominently in recent times. Performance of the States in terms of mobilisation of resources from their own sources has not been satisfactory due to many reasons, economic and non-economic. These factors have created acute problems for the fiscal adjustment in the States.

State's revenue receipts comprise of tax and non-tax revenues and transfers from the Centre. Taxes belonging exclusively to the

* This paper has been reproduced from the *Social Sciences Research Journal*, Chandigarh, Vol. 7, No. 1-2. The permission given by the Editor-in-Chief is gratefully acknowledged.

State by and large are the following : (i) land revenue, (ii) sales tax, (iii) State excise duty, (iv) stamps and registration duty, (v) income tax on agricultural land, (vi) taxes on passengers and goods carried on inland waterways, (vii) taxes on land and buildings, (viii) mineral rights, (ix) electricity duty, (x) entertainment tax. There are also some minor taxes such as, taxes on animals and boats, on road vehicles on advertisements, on luxuries and amusements etc., taxes on entry of good into local areas, tolls, fees in respect of the matters mentioned in State list. Taxes on professions, trades, etc. are also in the purview of States. Non-tax revenue consists of interest receipts and dividends, public works, irrigation, forests, administrative services, social and developmental services etc.

Share in Central taxes as determined by the successive Finance Commissions for every five years include mostly shares of income tax and Union excise duties. In addition to Finance Commission's devolution, States receive plan transfers from the Planning Commission, earlier under the Gadgil formula and now under the modified Gadgil Formula. States also receive certain grants under the centrally sponsored schemes from the individual ministries. Even after such Central transfers, the resources of the States are often found to be far from adequate to meet their expenditure needs.

This paper attempts to study the trend of revenue mobilisation in Orissa State in relation to other States in India. For a better perspective, the revenue receipts of the State have been analysed for two periods *viz.*, 1970-71 to 1980-81 and 1980-81 to 1996-97. The first section dwells upon the general trend of the revenue mobilisation of the State. The second section enumerates the tax effort of the State. In section III, the issue of slide down in mobilisation of non-tax revenue has been analysed and the section IV gives the conclusion.

SECTION I

Trends of Revenue Receipts of the State

Total revenue receipts (tax plus non-tax revenues) of the State has shown a trend of slow growth process over the period covered by the study. The trends clearly indicate that the growth rate in the second period is relatively lower than that of the first period. For instance, the average growth rate for the period 1970-71 to 1980-81 works out to 16.36 per cent per year against 13.20 per cent for the period 1980-81 to 1996-97 (see table 1).

The growth rate of total tax revenue has declined, though marginally, in the second period compared to the first period. The growth rate was 14.93 per cent during 1970-71 to 1980-81, which has declined to 14.58 per cent during 1980-81 to 1996-97. Both the components of tax revenue *i.e.,* own tax and share in Central taxes have shown lower growth rate in the second period. The average compound growth rate of own tax revenue, during the period 1970-71 to 1980-81 was 14.66 per cent as against 14.36 per cent during the period 1980-81 to 1996-97. In the case of share in Central taxes the growth rate was found to be 15.05 per cent during the period 1970-71 to 1980-81 and the same has gone down to 14.79 per cent during 1980-81 to 1996-97.

Now about the trends in non-tax revenues of the State : Total non-tax revenue, in terms of its growth rate, has declined substantially thus affecting the growth rate of total revenues of Orissa State. Growth rate of non-tax revenue has gone down to 11.39 per cent in the second period compared to the growth rate of 17.60 per cent in the earlier period (table 1). Such a steep decline in the growth rate of non-tax revenue in the State is due to sharp reduction in the growth rates of not only its components namely, own non-tax revenues, but also the grants from the Centre. The growth rate of own non-tax revenue of the State has declined from 17.93 per cent during the period 1970-71 to 1980-81 to 11.61 per cent for the period 1980-81 to 1996-97. Similarly, the growth rate of grants from the Centre has gone down from 17.50 per cent to 11.27 per cent during the same period. In the decade of eighties the growth rate of revenue receipts are modest. One striking factor is regarding the difference between the tax and non-tax receipts, the latter going down steeply in the second period.

From the shares in tax and non-tax revenues as also the grants, it can be observed that Central transfers (tax and non-tax revenues) contribute a significant proportion of the total revenues of the State (see table 2). Throughout the period covered by the study, the share in Central taxes and grants from Centre have been more than the own tax and own non-tax, tax share, receipts of the State. From figure 1, where absolute amount of own tax, tax share, own non-tax and grants are plotted, it can be seen that, the share in Central taxes is a major source of revenue throughout the period. The grants, after 1985 have shown higher growth than the own tax revenue. It is the own non-tax revenue of the State, which depicts a continuously low level growth throughout the period. This trend points out to a higher dependence of the State

TABLE 1

Growth Rate of Revenue Receipts of Orissa

(Per cent)

	Current Prices			Constant Prices		
	1970-71 to 1980-81	1980-81 to 1996-97	1970-71 to 1996-97	1970-71 to 1980-81	1980-81 to 1996-97	1970-71 to 1996-97
1. Total Revenue	16.36	13.20	13.79	9.13	5.68	5.56
2. Total Tax Revenue	14.93	14.58	14.82	7.70	6.83	6.79
3. Total Non-Tax Revenue	17.60	11.39	12.16	10.37	4.33	4.14
4. Share in Central Taxes	15.05	14.79	15.63	7.82	7.07	7.33
5. State's Own non-Tax Revenue	17.93	11.61	11.66	10.70	3.19	3.07
6. Grant-in-Aid	17.50	11.27	12.41	10.26	4.97	4.70
7. State's own Tax Revenue	14.66	14.36	14.75	7.43	6.54	6.24
7.1 Sales Tax	15.89	15.07	15.10	8.65	6.82	6.53
7.2 State Excise Duty	7.18	14.23	12.64	0.05	6.11	3.85
7.3 Tax on Vehicles and Goods	13.49	14.68	14.04	6.20	6.63	6.45
7.4 Land Revenue	14.21	13.73	14.09	6.98	8.45	6.56
7.5 Stamps and Registration duty	10.76	13.35	12.70	3.53	5.71	4.25
7.6 Electricity Duty	18.48	12.09	15.87	11.23	5.22	1.10
7.7 EntertainmentTax	18.47	2.87	8.84	11.25	5.44	8.31

Source : "Finances of State Governments" *RBI Bulletin*, Various Issues.

on Central devolution than its own sources. On the face of declining Central transfers to Orissa, the State should strive for exploiting its own resources. Generation of more resources internally gives a State autonomy and flexibility in decision making.

Taxes on vehicles and goods, produced a revenue of Rs. 3.79 crores in 1970-71 which has increased to Rs. 12.04 crores in 1980-81, Rs. 52.37 crores in 1990-91 and Rs. 128.23 crores in 1996-97. Its share in own tax revenue of the State was 11.39 per cent in 1970-71 which eventually came down to 9.12 per cent in 1980-81 and stood at 9.58 per cent in 1996-97.

Own Resources and Transfers to Orissa

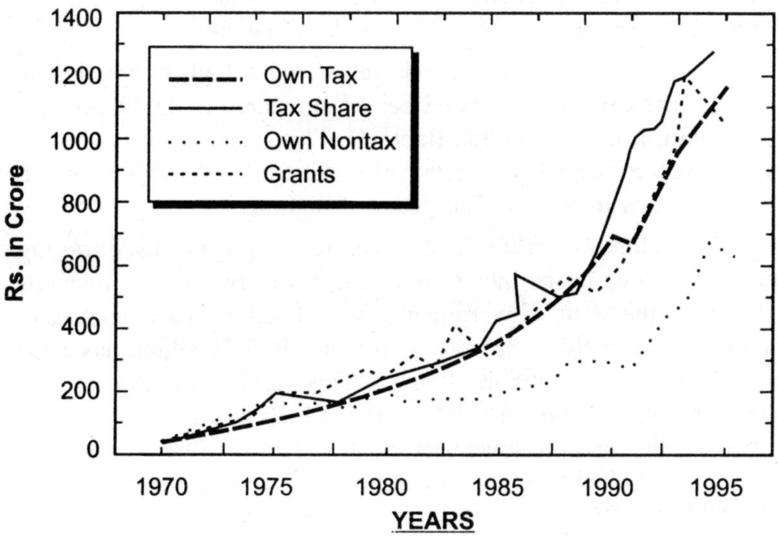

FIGURE 1

Trends of Individual Own Taxes

Among State's own taxes, sales tax is the major source of revenue earning. Sales tax revenue has increased substantially from Rs. 17.54 crores in 1970-71 to Rs. 76.63 crores in 1980-81 and to Rs. 893.51 crores in 1996-97. Share of sales tax in State's own tax revenue, has gone up from 52.72 per cent in 1970-71 to 58.02 per cent in 1980-81 and 66.58 per cent 1996-97 (table 3). Growth rate of sales tax has shown a decline in the second period compared to the earlier period (table 1). Its growth rate has come down from 15.89 per cent per annum during the period, 1970-71 to 1980-81 to 15.07 per cent per annum during the second period (*i.e.,* 1980-81 to 1996-97).

The revenue receipts from State excise has started growing only in the eighties. Its growth rate has improved from 7.18 per cent per annum during the period 1970-71 to 1980-81 to 14.23 per cent per annum during the period 1980-81 to 1996-97 (table 1). However, its share in own tax revenue has gone down from 12.77 per cent to 1970-71 to 6.76 in 1996-97.

Taxes on vehicles and goods registered a higher growth rate of 14.68 per cent in the second period compared to 13.49 per cent per annum in the first period (table 1). This increase in the growth rate however, helped it to retain the share of 8 to 9 per cent in the own taxes in most of the years of eighties.

The collection from land revenue was very discouraging initially but due to the inclusion of a cess on royalties on minerals (1985) by the State Government, the collections have increased. Land revenue yielded Rs. 1.67 crores in 1970-71 which has gone up only Rs. 6.47 crores in 1980-81. This yield from land revenue has gone up to the amount of Rs. 81.90 crores in 1990-91. However, the cess on minerals was abolished in 1991 on the basis of Supreme Court order. The land revenue, consequently has declined to Rs. 35.20 crores in 1996-97; which is even less than half of the 1990-91 collections. Its share in own taxes was 5.02 per cent in 1970-71 which came down to 4.17 per cent in 1980-81 and further to 2.62 per cent in 1996-97. The growth rate of land revenue, has gone down from 14.21 per cent in the period of 1970-71 to 1980-81 to 13.73 per cent per annum in 1980-81 to 1996-97.

The share of stamps and registration fees was 8.00 per cent in own tax revenue of the State in 1970-71, which came down to 5.92 per cent in 1980-81 and further to 5.11 per cent in 1996-97. Stamps and registration fees have achieved a higher

TABLE 2

Share of Various Sources of Revenue in Total Revenue of Orissa

(Per cent)

Year	Total Tax	Total Non-Tax	State's Own Tax	Share in Central Tax	State's Own Non-Tax	Grants-in-Aid
1970-71	53.26	46.74	27.81	25.46	14.20	32.54
1971-72	53.62	46.38	25.72	27.90	13.59	32.78
1972-73	48.78	51.22	23.76	25.02	22.51	28.71
1973-74	50.75	49.25	24.17	26.58	23.95	25.30
1974-75	42.96	57.04	22.18	20.78	21.13	38.55
1975-76	46.81	53.19	24.66	22.15	20.95	32.25
1976-77	44.82	55.18	24.81	20.02	23.94	31.24
1977-78	41.52	58.48	22.71	18.81	22.04	36.54
1978-79	38.90	61.10	21.99	16.91	21.21	39.89
1979-80	54.85	45.15	23.97	30.87	13.10	32.05
1980-81	47.01	52.99	21.26	25.75	21.57	31.42
1981-82	56.60	43.40	26.55	30.05	16.43	26.97
1982-83	46.27	53.73	21.66	24.61	13.02	40.71
1983-84	51.11	45.89	25.66	28.45	16.18	29.71
1984-85	62.21	37.79	27.68	34.53	14.71	23.08
1985-86	59.67	40.33	30.39	29.29	13.88	26.44
1986-87	61.25	38.75	27.51	33.74	12.89	25.87
1987-88	59.18	40.82	29.01	30.17	11.71	29.11
1988-89	56.19	43.81	28.55	27.64	12.46	31.35
1989-90	63.04	36.96	30.21	32.89	11.41	25.54
1990-91	62.78	37.22	30.81	31.97	9.26	27.96
1991-92	61.46	38.54	27.53	33.94	10.62	27.92
1992-93	60.30	39.70	26.15	34.15	13.32	26.37
1993-94	61.10	39.90	26.81	33.29	12.95	26.95
1994-95	53.98	46.02	23.72	30.26	15.82	30.20
1995-96	60.34	39.66	28.94	31.40	14.15	25.51

Source : Same as table 1.

growth rate to 13.35 per cent per annum in the second period, compared to 10.76 per cent per annum in seventies which made it possible for more than 5 per cent share in own taxes during the period 1980-81 to 1996-97.

Entertainment tax, which was expected to garner a sizeable amount of revenue for the State, came as a big disappointment. Its share in own taxes was 1.47 per cent in 1970-71, which has improved to 2.29 per cent in 1980-81 and came down sharply to only 0.43 per cent in 1996-97. The performance of entertainment tax was the poorest as its growth rate dipped to very low of 2.87 per cent during 1980-81 to 1996-97 from 18.47 per cent per annum during 1970-71 to 1980-81. So far as the electricity duty is concerned, which is a tax on electricity rates, performed better. It has grown from a low figure of Rs. 2.79 crores in 1970-71 to Rs. 16.92 per cent in 1980-81 and to Rs. 120.06 crores in 1996-97. The share of electricity duty in total taxes shows varied figures throughout the period. However, its share in own taxes was 8.39 per cent in 1970-71 which went up to 12.01 per cent in 1980-81 and came down to 8.95 per cent in 1996-97 (table 3). The growth rate of electricity duty has declined to 12.09 per cent in the second period from 18.48 per cent in the first period (table 1) which resulted in a decline of its share in total taxes.

The growth of tax revenue in the State in the recent times has been subdued. The slow growth of sales tax, which forms more than 60 per cent of own tax revenue is clear indicator of fledging fiscal performance of the State.

Per Capita Revenue Receipts

Per capita revenue receipts of 15 major States in selected years are given in table 4. From the per capita receipts figures, it is seen that, per capita own tax of Orissa has been lower than that of most of the States except Bihar and Assam. The per capita own tax revenue of Orissa was only Rs. 391.85 in 1996-97, the highest being Rs. 1418.73 of Gujarat followed by States like Maharastra, Tamil Nadu and Punjab. States like Karnatata, Kerala, Haryana and Andhra Pradesh have made great strides in increasing their per capita own tax revenues, whereas Orissa has not been able to increase its own tax revenues substantially.

The per capita total revenue (*i.e.*, tax plus non-tax) of Orissa has remained lower than many of the States throughout the period covered by the study. For instance, in 1996-97, the per capita

TABLE 3

Share of Own Taxes of State in the Total Own Taxes

(Per cent)

Year	Sales Tax	State Excise Duty	Vehicles & Goods	Land Revenue	Stamps & Regis-tration	Enter-tainment Duty	Electri-city Duty
1970-71	52.72	12.77	11.39	5.02	8.00	1.47	8.39
1971-72	50.37	13.40	8.82	5.16	9.25	1.87	11.12
1972-73	55.59	12.32	10.81	5.11	8.21	1.98	8.26
1973-74	53.25	12.06	11.37	5.50	8.22	1.66	7.80
1974-75	54.15	10.93	12.16	4.82	8.69	2.30	6.84
1975-76	55.61	8.96	11.21	4.66	7.67	1.93	9.84
1976-77	58.24	8.28	9.59	5.43	6.38	2.15	9.84
1977-78	56.13	8.34	10.35	5.75	6.70	2.26	10.15
1978-79	56.73	7.31	10.09	5.56	6.67	2.13	12.14
1979-80	58.83	6.98	9.86	4.17	6.43	2.52	11.20
1980-81	58.02	6.94	9.12	4.90	5.92	2.29	12.01
1981-82	59.07	6.90	8.38	3.29	5.81	2.19	14.39
1982-83	58.78	7.53	8.96	2.87	6.21	2.24	13.40
1983-84	56.74	7.68	9.25	4.45	6.23	1.97	13.69
1984-85	55.42	8.22	11.42	2.59	6.28	1.82	14.24
1985-86	51.89	7.57	9.74	5.57	6.04	1.77	17.42
1986-87	52.14	6.76	9.48	6.16	6.02	1.63	17.82
1987-88	53.28	6.86	9.12	7.80	5.74	1.40	15.80
1988-89	53.83	6.99	8.64	8.04	5.79	1.25	15.45
1989-90	56.14	7.28	8.36	15.01	5.32	0.96	6.35
1990-91	53.02	6.82	7.83	12.25	4.63	0.69	14.77
1991-92	58.51	8.17	8.87	3.68	5.26	0.74	14.76
1992-93	59.33	8.24	10.12	3.56	5.33	0.64	12.78
1993-94	59.81	8.86	10.05	3.66	5.58	0.58	11.45
1994-95	62.66	6.44	10.30	3.36	5.78	0.56	10.77
1995-96	63.52	6.52	9.54	3.50	5.59	0.56	10.77
1996-97	66.58	6.76	9.58	2.62	5.11	0.43	8.95

Sources : Same as table 1.

TABLE 4

Per Capita Revenue Receipts of States

(Per cent)

States	Total Revenue			Own Tax Revenue		
	1980-81	1990-91	1996-97	1980-81	1990-91	1996-97
1. A.P.	238.25	838.47	1561.39	109.67	415.11	680.98
2. Assam	285.97	716.97	1543.50	33.50	169.55	306.99
3. Bihar	142.70	503.67	837.75	39.94	133.04	234.59
4. Gujarat	264.49	829.49	2189.02	137.02	589.07	1418.73
5. Haryana	359.52	1172.73	3392.22	182.84	655.52	1201.97
6. KTA	259.44	864.37	1981.56	129.21	518.01	1187.83
7. Kerala	252.99	803.17	1975.53	132.96	448.01	1253.30
8. MP	219.15	712.97	1385.17	74.58	275.40	567.60
9. MHA	327.33	1162.52	2269.68	181.54	684.19	1380.88
10. Orissa	237.06	695.21	1251.65	50.39	214.17	391.85
11. Punjab	341.39	1002.53	2600.57	206.78	655.31	1277.10
12. Rajasthan	222.64	826.72	1521.10	68.09	275.64	628.54
13. TN	265.64	906.91	2018.51	132.64	556.86	1347.24
14. UP	173.12	614.16	1042.18	58.83	233.70	410.02
15. WB	201.74	627.73	1119.78	95.00	325.94	579.67

RANKS

State	Ranks : Total Revenue		Ranks : Own Tax	
	1980-81	1996-97	1980-81	1996-97
1. A.P.	9	8	8	8
2. Assam	4	9	15	14
3. Bihar	15	15	14	15
4. Gujarat	6	4	4	1
5. Haryana	1	1	2	6
6. Karnataka	7	7	7	7
7. Kerala	8	6	5	5
8. MP	12	11	10	11
9. Maharastra	3	3	3	2
10. Orissa	10	12	13	13
11. Punjab	2	2	1	4
12. Rajasthan	11	10	11	9
13. TN	5	5	6	3
14. UP	14	14	12	12
15. WB	13	13	9	10

Source : *RBI Bulletins* and *State's Economy* in figures, DES, Government of Orissa.

revenue receipts of Orissa stood at Rs. 1251.65, whereas the highest was that of Haryana at Rs. 3392.22 and the lowest, Rs. 837.75 in the case of Bihar. The States have been ranked on the basis of their per capita total revenue and per capita own taxes at two points of time *i.e.,* 1980-81 and 1996-97, which is presented in table 4. In the case of per capita total revenue and per capita own taxes, it is seen that Orissa remains at the bottom. The State occupies 13th position in regard to per capita own tax revenue in both the period and in the case of per capita total revenue, its rank has gone down from 10 to 12 over the same time period.

SECTION II

Buoyancy and Elasticity of Own Tax Revenue

Tax revenue depends upon its base and any possible changes in tax rate. If certain rate changes are introduced, they are known as 'discretionary changes' Normally, for many taxes, the base is the State Domestic Product. In other words, if the NSDP increases, the tax revenue also increases as it is understood that tax revenue is a function of State income. Buoyancy coefficient represents the increase in tax revenue on account of not only increase in the NSDP but also due to discretionary changes. If the tax series is cleaned for discretionary changes, we get, what is known as 'elasticity' of the tax with respect to changes in NSDP (*i.e.,* tax base).

For calculating the elasticity coefficients, the yearly gross tax revenue data are initially adjusted for the respective year's discretionary changes and further for the cumulative effects of the previous years' discretionary changes. The reconstruction of the tax revenue series has been done by following data adjustment method, suggested by Prest (1962). The methodology seeks to accommodate both rate and base changes. The Prest method suggests the derivation of the adjusted data from raw data in the following manner :

Let (a) T_1, T_2,.......T_i,.......T_n be the actual tax yields for a series of years.

(b) D_1, D_2,.......D_i,.......D_n be the estimate of revenue effects of discretionary changes tried over the corresponding years; and

(c) T_{ij} represents the J_{th} year's actual tax yield adjusted to the tax structure that existed in year i.

Then if i = 1 is taken as the reference year, the series T_{11}, T_{12},.......T_{1i},.....T_{1n} represent what the tax receipts would have been if the tax structure had remained as in the year 1, with all discretionary changes removed from the years following year 1. The procedure for adjustment takes the following form :

$$T_{11} = T_1$$
$$T_{12} = T_2 - D_2$$
$$T_{13} = T_{23}(T_{12}/T_2)$$
$$T_{14} = T_{34}\ (T_{23}/T_2)(T_{12}/T_2)$$
$$T_{ij} = T_{j-ij}\ (T_{j-2j-1}/T_{j-1})(..)........(T_{23}/T_3)(T_{12}/T_2)$$

This means; to adjust the tax yield of any year to the simulated yield for the year, if a base year tax structure had prevailed, the actual tax yield is to be multiplied by a sequence of multiplicative factors. The effect of each one of these is to adjust tax yields to the tax structure that prevailed in the year for which the factor refers to.

To estimate the buoyancy and the elasticity coefficients for the individual own taxes, the following equations are used.

$$\log T = \log a + b \log Y + u \qquad (1)$$
$$\log AT = \log a + b_i \log Y + v \qquad (2)$$

Where T = Actual tax revenue; AT = Adjusted tax revenue; Y = Net State Domestic Product and u and v are error terms. The coefficient, b, in equation (1) gives buoyancy and b_1, in equation (2) gives elasticity of tax structure.

Buoyancy and elasticity of taxes could be taken as indicators of over all performance of tax structure of the State. In this context, additional resource mobilisation of the State becomes important because different taxes behave in different ways while responding to various policy measures. The growth of the tax revenue corresponding to the growth of the State income is captured by the buoyancy coefficient. But elasticity shows the response of tax revenue to the automatic change in State income which, in other words, represents the built-in-flexibility of the tax system itself.

The buoyancy and elasticity coefficients of individual own taxes are given in table 5. The whole period under study has been divided into two phases, one, from 1970-71 to 1980-81 and second from 1980-81 to 1995-96, for assessing the responsiveness of the tax structure to change in NSDP. From the regression results, it is seen that, all the individual own taxes (except State

TABLE 5

Buoyancy and Elasticity Coefficients of State's Own Taxes

	Buoyancy Coefficients of Own Taxes							
Own Taxes	1970-71 to 1980-81				1980-81 to 1996-97			
	Buoyancy	R^2	DW	T	Buoyancy	R^2	DW	T
1. Total Own Tax	1.30	0.84	1.39	7.36	1.20	0.97	1.46	22.37
2. Sales Tax	1.40	0.83	1.49	7.12	1.25	0.98	1.94	30.44
3. Excise Duty	0.65	0.89	1.59	9.39	1.21	0.96	1.26	18.24
4. Vehicles and Goods	1.22	0.85	1.54	7.73	1.23	0.97	2.11	24.78
5. Land Revenue	1.27	0.83	0.98	7.02	1.24	0.55	0.73	4.42
6. Stamps and Registration Duty	0.96	0.84	1.72	7.46	1.13	0.98	5.53	31.77
7. Electricity Duty	1.60	0.73	1.25	5.36	1.04	0.81	1.96	7.94
8. Entertainment Tax	1.62	0.81	1.90	6.62	0.25	0.51	0.61	4.07

Elasticity Coefficients of Own Taxes

Own Taxes	1970-71 to 1980-81				1980-81 to 1996-97			
	Buoyancy	R^2	DW	T	Buoyancy	R^2	DW	T
1. Total Own Tax	0.91	0.79	1.35	6.25	0.77	0.91	1.79	11.73
2. Sales Tax	1.07	0.81	1.59	6.42	0.78	0.92	1.73	12.23
3. Excise Duty	0.40	0.78	1.99	6.13	0.59	0.83	1.97	8.08
4. Vehicles and Goods	1.04	0.86	1.68	8.05	0.88	0.92	2.58	12.49
5. Land Revenue	1.21	0.81	0.96	6.61	0.39	0.51	0.80	3.80
6. Stamps and Registration Duty	0.87	0.83	1.73	6.69	0.87	0.95	1.34	16.22
7. Electricity Duty	0.23	0.51	1.10	3.06	0.43	0.45	2.76	3.29
8. Entertainment Tax	0.92	0.73	1.79	5.02	0.08	0.41	0.58	1.59

Source : *RBI Bulletins* and Net States Domestic Product, CSO.

excise duty and stamps and registration duty in the first period and entertainment tax in second period), are buoyant in both the periods, as reflected by the values of their coefficients. The buoyancy coefficients during the second period have come down when compared to the first period.

The buoyancy of total own tax revenue of the State has come down from 1.30 in the first period to 1.20 in the second period. The sales tax shows a buoyancy coefficient of 1.40 in the period 1970-71 to 1980-81, which has come down to 1.25 per cent in the second period. Excise duty shows a very low buoyancy coefficient of 0.65 in the first period which has improved to 1.21 in the subsequent period. The low growth rate of excise duty in the first period has been reflected in its buoyancy. Stamps and registration duty shows a higher buoyancy coefficient of 1.13 in the second period compared to the earlier period. In the case of tax on vehicles and goods, the buoyancy coefficient has slightly improved from 1.22 to 1.23. The buoyancy in the case of land revenue, entertainment tax and electricity duty have gone down in the second period.

From the regression results, it is seen that the State's own tax as a whole is inelastic as the elasticity coefficient of total own tax is less than one. The coefficient is 0.91 during 1970-71 to 1980-81 and 0.77 during the period 1980-81 to 1995-96. This could mean that, the automatic response of tax system as a whole is less than proportionate to an increase in the State income. For other individual own taxes, namely, the sales tax, taxes on vehicles and goods and land revenue, the values of elasticity coefficients are more than one during the period 1970-71 to 1980-81, but eventually the same have gone down to less than one during the period 1980-81 to 1995-96, the elasticity coefficients for all taxes except excise and electricity duty, have gone down in the second period *i.e.,* in 1980-81 to 1995-96 compared to the period 1970-71 to 1980-81.

Relative Tax Effort of the States and the Position of Orissa

Tax effort of a Government can be understood as a relationship (ratio) between the amount of its tax collection and some measure of taxable capacity. In an economy the overall tax revenue should have a reasonable rate of growth. Tax effort, in the context is an important tool to assess the tax capability and the level of present effort. Measuring absolute tax effort in a cross section of States may not be possible due to the unreliability of the fixed taxable base for all the States. Rather, a relative tax effort measurement is more suitable to study fiscal performance across the States.

In the federation, tax effort of the State could be judged in relation to other States, or more specifically, in relation to the average performance of the States. The commonly used indicator of relative tax effort is the ratio of tax revenue to the total income of the State which is called 'tax ratio.' The use of tax ratio as an indicator of tax effort is not free from conceptual problems. It involves the implicit assumption that total income, irrespective of other circumstances, is the appropriate measure of taxable capacity. As a relative measure, revenue collection depends on the size of income in relation to population, degree of monetisation and the type of 'tax handles' available and like.

Tax effort of the States has been recognised by Planning Commission and Finance Commission to evaluate fiscal performance of the State and it serves as one of the criteria on the basis which transfer of tax shares and Central Plan grants are made.

Tenth Finance Commission has fixed 10 per cent of income tax and 8.42 per cent of basic excise duties to be shared with States on the basis of tax effort of the State. The Gadgil formula followed by the Planning Commission in allocation the Central share of State plan outlay, since Fourth Plan gives a 10 per cent weightage to the tax effort of the States, tax ratio being the criteria of tax effort (In recent revised allocation formula, tax effort as such is not included). Tax effort, could be taken as an attempt at estimating normative yields from the tax basis, *i.e.,* State income. The tax bases instead of using State income only, can be extended in more detail, to the individual tax bases to find the taxable capacity and compare it with actual revenue generated.

In the fiscal policy of the States, tax effort seeks to mobilise more revenue, with the expansion of the economy and resulting rise in taxable capacity. Introduction of new taxes and changes in the base of the tax structure, administrative improvements are various aspects that help in raising the tax effort. Two measures are used here to evaluate the relative tax effort of the State in general and Orissa State in particular. First, comparison of State's own tax with SDP, *i.e.,* 'tax ratio' and second an inter-State comparison of actual tax ratios (T/Y) with a presumptive tax ratio estimated by aggregate regression method. The aggregate regression method for measuring the tax effort has been used in studies like Lotz and Morss (1969), Chelliah (1971), Bahl (1971).

Inter-State Comparison of Tax Income Ratio

In table 6, ratio of own tax revenue and State income of 15 major States in India for various years and all States' average of tax ratio for the same years are presented. From the tax-income ratios given in both the periods, it can be seen that, State like

TABLE 6

State-wise Comparison of Tax-Income Ratio (T/Y)

(Per cent)

States	1970-71	1980-81	1985-86	1990-91	1995-96
A.P.	5.35	7.95	10.95	8.49	6.64
Assam	3.37	2.86	4.56	4.42	4.59
Bihar	3.43	4.36	4.65	5.00	5.05
Gujarat	4.94	8.11	8.88	9.88	10.76
Haryana	5.06	7.71	8.67	8.74	8.67
Karnataka	5.39	8.50	10.53	11.33	12.24
Kerala	5.16	8.80	11.23	11.01	13.63
MP	4.35	5.47	6.88	6.61	7.35
Maharastra	6.59	7.45	8.60	8.89	8.31
Orissa	3.20	3.84	4.59	6.92	5.39
Punjab	5.99	7.84	8.03	7.69	7.73
Rajasthan	3.66	5.58	7.38	6.78	8.10
TN	6.19	8.85	11.31	11.09	12.40
UP	3.59	4.60	5.23	6.39	6.06
WB	4.10	5.36	6.45	6.72	7.16
All States	4.38	6.00	7.01	7.13	7.29

Source : *RBI Bulletins* (Various Issues) and Net State Domestic Product, CSO.

Tamil Nadu, Kerala, Maharastra, Karnataka, Haryana, Punjab, Gujarat and Andhra Pradesh have recorded rates more that all States' average, Assam being at the bottom. Orissa's performance in terms of tax ratio is not at all satisfactory. In the case of Orissa, the deviation from all State's average has been quite high. The tax ratio for Orissa works out to be 3.20 per cent in 1970-71 which has improved to 5.39 per cent in 1995-96. Tax ratio of Orissa is way below the all State's average 7.25 per cent in that year. The improvement in tax ratio for Orissa over a period of one decade seems modest. Among all the States, the State's performance in terms of tax ratio has been one of the lowest.

Actual and Presumptive Tax-Income Ratio

Relative tax efforts of the States could be found by comparing actual tax-income ratio with presumptive tax-income ratio. Presumptive tax-income ratio is an average response to such tax handles as are available, which in other words, are bases of taxes. Looking at the difficulty in finding comparable bases for each tax across the States, proxies for such purpose could be taken which would form potential bases. Sectoral incomes and per capita income of States are taken as potential bases for State taxes which indicate the taxable capacity. A multiple regression of following type is run to find out the average response of tax handles.

$$TY = a + b_1YA + b_2YM + b_3YS + b_4YN + U \quad (1)$$

where, YA = share of agriculture in NSDP

YM = share of manufacturing in NSDP

YS = share of services in NSDP

YN = per capita income.

The tax on agriculture being negligible in almost all the States, the income from agriculture is best excluded from the equation. However, the income generated from processing of agricultural commodities enter into the industrial sector. The regression coefficient of per capita income is found to be statistically insignificant and, therefore, per capita income (YN) has been dropped. Later with remaining variables, the regression has been carried out. The equation takes the following form :

$$TY = a + b_1YM + b_2YS + U \quad (2)$$

After estimating the equation the values of independent variables are plugged in the equation for all the States to calculate the respective presumptive tax-income ratios. Dividing the actual tax-income ratio by the presumptive ratio an index was found to compare the tax effort of the States.

To estimate the above equation, average values of tax and sectoral income for three years from 1993-94 to 1995-96 were taken for each State. The results obtained from the multiple regression based on the equation (2) are given below :

$$TY = -3.5581 + \underset{(2.7395)}{0.2228YM} + \underset{(1.8902)}{0.1615YS} \quad (3)$$

$R^2 = 0.50$, DW = 1.42

(figures in brackets are t values)

The relevant values are plugged in the equation (2) for 15 States under study and the estimated tax-income ratio are found. Here one point should be noted regarding the equation (2). To capture the changes in the tax-income ratio, more variables like exact bases for the State taxes could be introduced to find better results. Due to severe difficulty in getting such comparable bases for each tax across the 15 States, this equation is used which would serve our purpose of comparing the tax effort of the States in India.

Actual tax-income ratio, estimated tax income ratio and the ratio of actual and estimated tax income ratio of States are presented in table 7. From the Table it can be seen that, States like Haryana, Karnataka, Kerala, Punjab, Rajasthan and Tamil Nadu have actual tax-income ratios which are more than the estimated tax-income ratios. Thus, the ratio of actual to estimated tax-income ratio, which is used as an index to compare the tax effort of the States, for these State is more than one. Other States have a lower actual tax-income ratio than the estimated ratio, thus resulting in lower tax effort index, which is less than one in each case. The States like Assam, Bihar, Uttar Pradesh, Orissa, Maharastra and West Bengal have performed below their tax potentials. Orissa has a tax effort index of 71 per cent which is less than most of the States, except Assam. Looking at the ranking of the States on the basis of the tax effort index, which is the

TABLE 7

Actual and Presumptive Tax-Income Ratio of Individual States (1993-94 to 1995-96)

States	T/Y	P/Y	(T/Y)/(P/Y)	Ranks
A.P.	7.35	7.64	0.96	8
Assam	4.54	6.55	0.69	15
Bihar	5.27	6.82	0.77	12
Gujarat	10.26	10.32	0.99	7
Haryana	8.67	7.18	1.21	4
Karnataka	11.53	7.82	1.47	1
Kerala	12.82	8.74	1.46	2
MP	7.08	7.65	0.93	8
Maharastra	8.30	11.27	0.74	13
Orissa	5.35	7.50	0.71	14
Punjab	7.94	6.45	1.23	3
Rajasthan	6.73	6.70	1.00	6
TN	11.58	11.14	1.04	5
UP	6.05	7.14	0.85	10
WB	7.01	8.29	0.84	11

Note : Actual tax-income ratio : T/Y.
Presumptive Tax-income Ratio : P/Y.

ratio of actual to estimated tax-income ratio, Karnataka is at the top position followed by Kerala and Punjab and Assam is at the lowest position. Orissa occupies the 14th position in the ranking of the States. It could therefore be concluded on the basis of tax effort analysis (by this method) for Orissa, that, there is still scope for the State to mobilise more revenue from its own tax sources.

The relationship between tax ratio and per capita income is an important aspect of any tax structure and the tax effort of the State should be seen from this angle also. A positive relation between tax ratio and per capita income refers to a wide base of the tax structure. Burgess and Stern (1993), estimated this relationship for 82 developing countries and pointed out that rise in tax ratio is related positively with per capita GNP. In the present study, we have estimated the above relationship by taking a total period of 27 years from 1970-71 to 1996-97 for the Orissa State. The equation takes the following form :

$$LTY = 0.0163+0.1995\ LPCI + u \qquad (4)$$
$$(6.2039)$$
$R^2 = 0.68$, $DW = 1.96$,
where LTY = log of tax ratio.
LPCI = log of per capita income

The positive coefficient in equation (4) shows the capacity of rising per capita income to improve the tax ratio. The low value of the coefficient (nearly 20 per cent), implies that per capita income did not influence much to improve the tax ratio in Orissa. This finding is, however, not consistent with the general idea that ability to tax grows faster than the income. Musgrave and Musgrave (1980) expressed that the 'handles' to which the revenue system may be attached become more diverse with economic development resulting in widening in the tax base. From tax effort analysis, it is seen that the effort of Orissa State in mobilising the tax revenue has not been satisfactory. The weak relationship between per capita income and tax ratio, only reinforces such finding.

SECTION III

Non-Tax Revenues in the State

Non-tax revenue should have an important place in the revenue receipts of Orissa State. Vast forest resources, sizeable mineral sources along with other returns from Government services have revenue generating potential in the State. Broadly, the own non-tax revenue could be divided into certain categories, *viz.*, interest receipts; receipts from dividends generated by public sector enterprise; returns from social, general and economic services. The grants from the Centre are also considered as non-tax revenue in the State's budget and are also a major part of the total revenues of Orissa. However, grants do not form a part of own non-tax revenue of the State. In the decade of eighties, non-tax revenue in the State has lost its importance compared to the tax revenues. The fiscal imbalance in the State has worsened over the years due to variety of reasons. An important fiscal adjustment difficulty for the State in the recent times has been the declining contribution of non-tax revenues.

State Governments invest in many public sector enterprises, irrigation, transport and other services on which users pay charges at very low rates. The charges are determined by the Government looking at the social objectives and their usefulness for economic

TABLE 8

Share of Non-Tax Receipts in Own Revenue of the State

(Per cent)

Year	Interest Receipts	Dividends	General Services	Social Services	Economic Services	Own Non-Tax Receipts
1970-71	23.83	0.20	1.69	10.07	1.99	37.78
1971-72	24.38	0.21	1.24	12.88	7.09	45.80
1972-73	16.71	0.13	3.96	2.84	25.00	48.64
1973-74	16.81	0.13	4.52	4.80	23.51	49.77
1974-75	19.37	0.18	2.78	3.31	23.14	48.78
1975-76	14.77	0.08	2.66	3.18	24.78	45.46
1976-77	16.06	0.07	5.84	3.78	23.35	49.11
1977-78	16.16	0.07	2.95	5.78	24.23	49.19
1978-79	14.91	0.05	2.89	3.64	27.60	49.09
1979-80	2.81	0.08	4.20	4.35	23.90	35.34
1980-81	3.21	0.07	23.89	2.61	20.57	50.37
1981-82	2.72	0.08	2.69	4.16	28.57	38.23
1982-83	4.74	0.08	2.47	3.99	26.27	37.55
1983-84	6.58	0.08	2.80	3.83	25.25	38.55
1984-85	6.18	0.05	3.10	3.09	22.27	24.70
1985-86	2.68	0.05	5.41	4.93	18.29	31.36
1986-87	2.52	0.04	6.81	4.09	18.45	31.90
1987-88	1.57	0.04	2.99	2.58	21.57	28.76
1988-89	2.43	0.03	6.92	0.56	18.44	30.39
1989-90	0.83	0.03	2.78	2.42	21.30	27.42
1990-91	0.97	0.01	2.52	2.58	17.04	23.12
1991-92	3.65	0.01	2.88	2.56	18.73	27.83
1992-93	5.07	0.10	4.03	2.42	22.14	33.75
1993-94	6.88	0.05	3.25	2.20	20.20	32.58
1994-95	3.45	0.01	3.02	1.89	32.39	40.74
1995-96	7.90	0.12	4.58	1.69	21.49	35.79
1996-97	0.74	0.02	2.67	1.93	21.06	26.41

Source : Same as table 1.

development. The investments made on economic services, social services are essential in order to meet the responsibilities entrusted upon them. Social services include providing health facility, education, urban development, etc. Expenditures on economic services encourage economic development in the State and a reasonable return on such services are expected. The charges on irrigation, transport, earnings from forests, fisheries, royalty on minerals rights are some of the non-tax receipts in economic services sector.

Looking at the various components of own non-tax (table 8) in terms of their shares in own revenue of the States it is found that in most of the cases a declining trend is perceived. The own non-tax receipts as percentage of own revenue of the State has declined to 26.41 per cent in 1996-97 from 37.78 per cent in 1970-71 and 50.37 per cent in 1980-81. The significance of non-tax revenue in recent time has suffered a set back. Looking at the share of dividends, it becomes apparent that, the revenue from State owned industries have become irrelevant. The returns from heavy investments in social sector is another area in which the picture has been very dismal. It is only the economic services, where the share has been sustained to some extent. However, compared to the figures in early eighties, the shares show a declining trend. The growth rates of individual non-tax receipts show a slowdown in the post 1980-81 scenario (see table 9).

Two important sources of non-tax revenue in Orissa have been the revenue from minerals and from forests. Forest revenues which generally come from sale of timber, kendu leaves and other forest products have been growing over the years. The revenue from forest has been increased from Rs. 5.57 crore in 1970-71 to Rs. 37.27 crores in 1980-81, Rs. 109.5 crores in 1990-91 and Rs. 118.21 crores in 1994-95. The ratio of revenue from forest products to that of its corresponding NSDP has declined during the period covered by the study. Share of revenues from forests out of the income generated in the corresponding sector of NSDP stood at 37.76 per cent in 1970-71, and the same has declined to 21.44 per cent in 1980-81 and to 17.44 per cent in 1995-96. It is necessary to take appropriate steps to arrest the declining trend of forest revenues. Royalties on minerals yielded Rs. 2.57 crore

TABLE 9

Growth Rate of Non-Tax Receipts

	1970-71 to 1980-81	1980-81 to 1995-96	1970-71 to 1995-96
1. Interest Receipts	- 1.48	11.29	3.88
2. Dividends	3.50	3.21	4.52
3. General Services	31.53	9.75	14.36
4. Social Services	7.09	8.49	9.06
5. Economic Services	31.39	12.92	15.70

Source : Same as table 1.

NOTES

(i) After 1980-81, the Government expenditure in most of the States including Orissa has picked up due to the fast rising revenue expenditure (see Bagchi *et al.*, 1992). Keeping that in view the trend of revenue receipts has been analysed here for two periods to ascertain the revenue effort in the eighties.

(ii) All the data relating to individual own taxes are taken from RBI Bulletins.

(iii) Plan allocation formula employed by the Planning Commission.

Items (Weightage %)	Original Gadgil Formula (1969)	Modified Formula (1980)	Latest Formula (1991)
Population	60	60	60
Tax Effort	10	10	-
Per Capita Income	10	20	25
Irrigation & Power Projects	10	-	-
Special Problems	10	10	7.5
Performance : Fiscal Mngt.	-	-	7.5

(iv) All statistics regarding income generated and revenue receipts from forestry and loging have been taken from "Statistical Abstracts" (various issues) published by Government of Orissa.

in 1974-75 which was improved to Rs. 8.01 crore in 1984-85. Subsequently, the royalty on minerals was included in the land revenue by the State Government. The State Government has tried to increase the royalties on minerals which was dismissed by the Supreme Court. This has created lot of strain on the revenues of the State. The Central Government should compensate adequately to the State Government on this account.

SECTION IV

Conclusion

Slow down in the growth rate of own revenues of the State has put severe strain on the overall financial position of the State. From the growth rates of the revenue sources of the State, it is observed that, in most cases, the growth rate has slowed down in the second period. Total tax revenue, which includes own taxes of the State and the share in Central taxes has shown a declined in growth rate in the second period. The growth rate of own taxes of the State has gone down from 14.66 per cent to 14.36 per cent per annum over the same periods. Total non-tax revenue has shown a steep decline in growth rate as the components of total non-tax, namely, own non-tax and grants from Centre have shown sharp decline in their growth rate. The performance on the tax mobilisation front could be termed as modest which does not suit to the overall development scenario.

From the per capita revenue figures across States, it is seen that, Orissa has one of the lowest per capita figures. Among the individual own tax revenue of the State, the growth rate of sales tax has come down from 15.89 per cent in the first period to 15.07 per cent per annum in the second period. The declining growth rate of sales tax starting from 1980-81 causes serious concern as 60 per cent of own taxes of the State has been generated through this tax only.

From the regression analysis to estimate the degree of responsiveness of the tax structure to the NSDP of the State, it is seen that, the State taxes are buoyant over the period covered by the study, but they are not elastic. In most of the cases, the buoyancy and elasticity coefficients are lower in the second period than that of the first period. Inelastic tax system in the State implies that, the mobilisation of additional resources depend more upon *ad hoc* policy measure than on an automatic response to rise in State income.

To estimate tax effort of the States, two measures, namely, tax ratio and aggregate regression approach have been followed. Tax-income ratio of the State has been calculated at various points of time starting from 1970-71. The tax ratio of Orissa has been one of the lowest except that of States like Bihar and Assam. While estimating tax effort of the States using aggregate regression approach, Orissa's rank was 14th in the period, 1993-94 to 1995-96 with tax effort index of 71 per cent. From the tax effort analysis, as is evident, the effort of Orissa State to exploit its own tax base has been inadequate. Lower tax ratio and tax effort index implies that the State has the scope for mobilisation of resources from its own sources.

Regarding own non-tax of the State its share in total revenues has declined substantially in the second period starting from 1980-81. The growth rate of own non-tax revenue of the State has come down from 17.93 per cent during the period 1970-71 to 1980-81, to 11.61 per cent per annum during the second period at current prices. The scope for mobilising revenue from non-tax revenue source are quite high in the case of Orissa. The declining non-tax revenue of the State calls for immediate attention to reinforce this important sources of revenue. The declining non-tax revenue could be traced to the loss making public sector enterprises, stagnation in royalties from minerals and earning from forestry and low rate of returns from the Government investments in economic, social and general services.

Though the demand for generating more revenues internally has been increasing, the effort of Orissa Government has been inadequate. The declining growth rate of tax, and non-tax revenues, during the period starting from 1980-81 to 1995-96 has contributed to the fiscal problem in the State. The per capita own tax receipts of Orissa State has been one of the lowest among major States in India. A comprehensive tax reforms in the State level with strict administration may be attempted to improve the present situation.

REFERENCES

ACIR (1962), *Measuring of State and Local Fiscal capacity and Tax Effort*, Washington, DC.

Akin, John, S. (1973), *Fiscal Capacity and the Estimation Methods of the Advisory Commission on Inter-Governmental Relation*, National Tax Journal, Vol. 26, No. 2.

Bagchi, Amaresh, J. L. Bajaj and William A. Byrd (ed.), (1992), *State Finances in India*, Vikas Publishing House Pvt. Ltd., New Delhi.

Bagchi Amaresh, Nicholas Stern (1994), *Tax Policy and Planning in Developing Countries*, Oxford University Press.

Bahl, R.W. (1971), "A Regression Approach to Tax Effort and Tax Ratio Analysis" *IMF Staff Papers*, Vol. 18, No.3, November, pp. 570-612 (1972), A Representative Tax System Approach to Measuring Tax effort in Developing Countries, *IMF Staff Papers*, Vol. 119, No. 1.

Bird, R.M. (1976), "Assessing Tax Performance in Developing Countries : A Critical Review of the Literature," *Finanzarchiv*, Vol. 34, No. 2.

—— (1993), "Tax reforms in India, Review Article," *Economic and Political Weekly*, Vol. 27, No. 50, Dec. 11, pp. 27, 21-26.

Bird, R.M. and Oliver Oldman (ed.), (1967), *Readings on Taxation in Developing Countries*, Hopkins, Baltimore.

Burgess, R. and Nicholas Stem (1993), *Taxation and Development*, Journal of Economic Literature, Vol. 31, June, pp. 762-830.

Burgess, R., Stephen Hower and Nicholas Stern (1995), "The Reform of Indirect Taxes in India," in Purohit, M.C. and V.K. Purohit, ed. (1995), *Commodity Taxes in India, Directions and reforms*, Gayatri Publication.

Chelliah, R.J. (1971), "Trends In Taxation in Developing Countries," *IMF Staff Papers*, Vol. 18, No. 2, July, pp. 154-331.

Jena, P.R. (1999), *State Finances of Orissa : A Temporal Study*, Unpublished Ph.D. Thesis, University of Hyderabad.

Lotz, J.R. and Elliot Morss (1967), "Measuring 'Tax Effort' in Developing Countries," *IMF Staff Papers*, Vol. 14, No. 3, November, pp. 478-499.

Marsden, Keith (1983), Links between Taxes and Economic Growth : Some Empirical Evidence, *World Bank Staff Working Papers*, No. 605, The World Bank, Washington.

Musgrave, R.A. and P. Musgrave (1980), *Public Finance in Theory and Practice*, Mcgraw Hill Ltd.

Oomen, M.A. (1987), Relative Tax Effort of States, *Economic and Political Weekly*, March.

Prest, A.R. (1962), "The Sensitivity of the Yield of the Personal Income Tax in the United Kingdom," *Economic Journal*, Vol. 72, Sept., pp. 576-596.

Rao, V.G. (1979), *The Responsiveness of the Indian Tax System* : 1960-61 to 1973-74, Allied Publishers Pvt. Ltd.

Sahota, G.S. (1961), *Indian Tax Structure and Economic Development*, Asia Publishing House, Bombay.

Sen, Tapas Kand V.B. Tulasidhar (1988), *Taxable Capacity and Tax Effort of States in India*, NIPEP, New Delhi.

Wallich, Christine (1982), State Finances in India, Studies in State Finances, *IMF Staff working papers*, Vol. 2, No. 523.

Wilford, W.T. (1965), "State Tax Stability Criteria and the Revenue Income Elastic Coefficient Reconsidered," *National Tax Journal*, Vol. 18, No. 13, Sept., pp. 304-312.

4

FINANCIAL STATUS OF STATES — THE STATE OF AFFAIRS IN M.P.*

—*S. Murty*

1. Introduction

The State of Madhya Pradesh emerged on 1st November 1956 as a sequel of the reorganization of States in India. Areas which form part of this State are seventeen districts of Mahakoshal, *viz.* Jabalpur, Sagar, Hoshangabad, Nimar, Mandala, Betul, Chhindwara, Raipur, Bilaspur, Durg, Bastar, Raigarh, Sarguja Balaghat, Seoni, Damoh and Narsinghpur, eight districts of previous Vindhya Pradesh, *viz.* Datia, Tikamgarh, Chhatarpur, Panna, Satna, Rewa, Sidhi and Shahdol, Sixteen districts of erstwhile Madhya Bharat (excluding Sunel enclaves) *viz.* Bhind, Morena, Shivpur, Guna, Vidisha, Rajgarh, Shajapur, Ujjain, Indore, Dewas, Ratlam, Dhar, Jhabua, Nimar and Mandsaur and the whole of Bhopal State consisting of two districts *viz.* Sehore and Raisen and the Sironj sub-division of Kota district in Rajasthan. Madhya Pradesh lies in the very heart of India, surrounded by seven States *viz.* U.P., Bihar, Orissa, Andhra Pradesh, Maharashtra, Gujarat and Rajasthan.

2. Economic Development of M.P.

The best measure of economic development is net domestic product and per capita income. The status of these in M.P. has been as shown in table 1.

* This paper pertains to erstwhile Madhya Pradesh State.

TABLE 1

Net State Domestic Product & Per Capita Income of M.P.

Year	Net State Domestic Product (in Crore Rs.)		Per Capita Income in Rupees	
	At Current Prices	At Constant Prices	At Current Prices	At Constant Prices
1	2	3	4	5
1960-61	831.8	831.8	260.1	260.1
1970-71	1091.3	1991.3	484.2	484.2
1980-81	6121.7	2675.0	1183.1	517.0
1990-91	23043.3	4876.1	3614.4	764.8
1997-98	54943.0	—	7445.0	—

Source : *Economic Survey of M.P.*, Directorate of Economics & Statistics, Bhopal.

The table shows that both the domestic product and per capita income are rising at current and constant prices. The rise of per capita income is lower in comparison to the rise of net domestic product due to fast growing population. During 1981-91, the growth rate of population in M.P. was 2.38 while it was 2.14 in India, taking up population by 6.62 crores in 10 years. In M.P., the S.C., S.T., population is about 34% and only 44.20% population is literate, whereas the national average is 52.21% for 1997. 40.6% people are below the poverty line which is 3% more than the national average.

3. Fiscal Status of M.P.

Government of M.P. issued a white paper in 1999 which showed the status of economic crisis in the State. This crisis is visible in the fiscal deficit of this year's budget also. Table 2 shows the position of budget for 3 years.

The table shows that the fiscal deficit has gone up from 1998-99 to 2000-2001, though the primary deficit was lower in this year in comparison to last year. If we look at the percentage rise in gross fiscal deficit, it came down by 0.05% in 1995-96. Thereafter it went on increasing by 36.7% in 1996-97, 22% in 1997-98, 65.3% in 1998-99, -4% in 1999-2000 and 5.5% in 1999-2000. Thus, the general trend is that of rising.

TABLE 2

Budget Position of M.P. (In Crore Rupees)

S.No.	Item	1998-99	1999-2000	2000-2001
01.	Revenue Receipts	11345.85	13804.79	14188.29
02.	Capital Receipts	3997.70	3525.49	3906.72
03.	Public Debt	2356.90	2370.39	2557.69
04.	Total Receipts (01+02)	15343.55	17330.28	18095.01
05.	Revenue Expenditure	14217.65	16420.22	17057.83
06.	Capital Expenditure	1009.89	1218.42	1094.63
07.	Total Expenditure	15227.54	17638.64	18152.46
08.	Revenue Deficit	-2871.80	-2615.43	-2869.54
09.	Fiscal Deficit	-4126.72	-3973.17	-4187.59
10.	Primary Deficit	-2291.97	-1718.58	-1583.56

Source : Annual Budgets of M.P.

4. Reasons for Fiscal Crisis

There are more than one reasons for the current fiscal crisis :

4.1 High Establishment Cost and Interest Payment

The establishment cost and cost of interest payment is going up every year in the State and a high amount of budget goes to these costs as shown in the following table :

TABLE 3

Establishment Expenses and Interest Payment in M.P. (In Crore Rupees)

Year	Establishment Expenditure	Interest Payment
1996-97	4635.69	1376.22
1997-98	5186.72	1659.92
1998-99	6864.26	1834.76

Source : Annual Budgets of M.P.

4.2 Increase in Non-Plan Expenditure

With every new plan one number of previous plans increases resulting in an increase in non-plan expenditure. When new plan is taken up, old plan can not be cancelled. Its establishment expenditure has to be carried out resulting in increase in non-plan expenditure with every subsequent plan. The following table shows the increasing percentage of non-plan expenditure in M.P.

TABLE 4

Percentage Increase in Non-Plan Expenditure in M.P.

Year	Percent Increase
1995-96	17.40
1996-97	18.00
1997-98	18.60
1998-99	90.20

Source : Annual Budget of M.P.

For the plan period, the Central Government gives aid to meet the plan expenditure of centrally sponsored activities but after the plan the responsibility comes on the shoulders of the State government. If the activity is a productive activity, like agriculture, industry or paying infrastructure activity, there is no problem but if the activity is unproductive social activity, the State Government does not get any or very less income from the activity and has to carry out the liability of establishment and other costs.

4.3 Increase in Unproductive Expenditure

There is a lot of unproductive expenditure in the state. Unnecessary meetings of officers, administrators and politicians, unnecessary tours of officials, administrators and politicians, unwieldy number of officials and politicians, necessary party's luncheons, increase in Government vehicles and telephones, unnecessary corporations, unnecessary seminars and conferences, unnecessary functions and anniversaries, duplication of policies, projects and programmes cause waste of money, time and energy and should be strictly curtailed.

4.4 Decentralization of Administration

Decentralization of administration has caused increase in the number of Government paid people and work channels, making things more complicated, less efficient and more slow and dilute.

4.5 Poor Tax Revenue

With increase in economic activities, production and income, the percentage of tax revenue should go up in the economy but the situation is not so.

TABLE 5

Percentage of Tax Revenue in M.P. and Other States

Year	M.P.	Other States
1991-92	12.80	16.50
1995-96	12.1	14.50
1996-97	16.60	11.30
1997-98	13.10	19.50
1998-99	12.80	18.20

Source : *Economic Times.*

The table shows that percentage of tax revenue during 1991-92 and in 1998-99 is 12.80 in M.P., whereas it is 16.50 in 1991-92 in other States and 18.20% in 1998-99 in other states. The percentage is not only more but has also increased.

4.6 Loss of Public Undertaking

Loss of public undertaking is a very important cause of financial crisis. In the year ending March 1996, the undertaking which made loss or profit were as under :

TABLE 6

Profit/Loss of Public Enterprises in M.P. (Year Ending, March 1998)

(Amount in Lakhs)

Sr. No.	Name of Public Enterprise	Profit	Loss	Amount (Rs. in Lakhs)
01.	M.P. Provident Investment Co., Mumbai	Profit		46.53
02.	M.P. Small Scale Industries Corporation	Profit		56.91
03.	M.P. State Industrial Development Corporation	Profit		338.34
04.	M.P. Civil Supplies Corporation	Profit		544.17
05.	M.P. State Forest Development Corporation	Profit		517.51
06.	M.P. State Export Corporation	Profit		481.00
07.	M.P. Electronics Department Corporation	Profit		865.65

Sr. No.	Name of Public Enterprise	Profit	Loss	Amount (Rs. in Lakhs)
08.	M.P. Finance Corporation, Indore	Profit		116.11
09.	M.P. Housing Board	Profit		1747.00
10.	M.P. State Ware Housing Corporation	Profit		384.62
11.	M.P. Seeds & Farm Development Corporation	Profit		78.00
12.	M.P. State Animal Husbandry and Poultry Development Corporation	Profit		50.01
13.	M.P. Women Economic Development Corporation	Profit		24.12
		Total Profit		5249.97
14.	M.P. Khadi & Rural Industries Board		Loss	40.05
15.	M.P. State Industries Corporation		Loss	945.21
16.	M.P. Mines Development Corporation		Loss	176.18
17.	M.P. State Agricultural Industries Dev. Corporation		Loss	88.57
18.	M.P. State Textile Corporation		Loss	957.92
19.	M.P. State Tourism Development Corporation		Loss	207.39
20.	M.P. Police Housing Department		Loss	128.45
21.	M.P. Leather Development Corporation		Loss	05.40
22.	M.P. Handicraft Development Corporation		Loss	40.35
23.	M.P. Film Development Corporation		Loss	10.09
24.	M.P. State Land Development Corporation		Loss	655.17
25.	M.P. State Fisheries Development Corporation		Loss	32.12
26.	M.P. Backward Class Finance & Development Corporation		Loss	09.69
27.	M.P. State Energy Development Corporation	No Profit No Loss		
28.	M.P. State Text Book Corporation	No Profit No Loss		
29.	M.P. Tribal Finance & Development Corporation	No Profit No Loss		
		Total	Loss	3296.59

Source : *Janmat Swar*, December, 1999.

The total profit is 5249.97 lakh rupees and total loss is 3296.59 lakh rupees. Thus, the net gain is only 1953.38 lakh rupees, which is very less in comparison to the heavy investment made in these corporations.

4.6 Revised Pay Scales

For the states, the fiscal burden was exacerbated due to the additional expenditure arising out of implementation of revised pay scales of State Government employees.

4.6 Structural Weaknesses

It is also seen that the fiscal position of both the Centre and States suffer from structural weaknesses — the former, due to a high level of non-plan expenditure, which forms almost three-fourth of aggregate expenditure and the latter as a result of limited resource base in contrast to the increasing expenditure commitments. This in turn, has raised issues of sustainability of domestic debt.

1. Conclusion and Solution

In the recent period, the need for introduction of a fiscal responsibility legislation has been gaining ground. Considering the fiscal strains that the Centre and State governments have been facing, especially in most recent times, it is logical to moot such proposal. The Report on Currency and Finance 1998-99 brought out by the RBI has amply highlighted the need for avoiding fiscal profligacy and more towards fiscal consolidation. According to the report, while the gross fiscal deficit (GFD) of the Central Government as per cent of Gross Domestic Product (GDP) in 1998-99 was 6.3%, the combined GFD of the Government sector (Centre and States) was as high as 8.5%. The slippage in major deficit indicators during 1998-99 was mainly as a result of revenue shortfalls due to a reduction in tax collections.

The issue of fiscal consolidation involves various complex factors, more so when the Central Bank (in case of India, it is the Reserve Bank of India) is primarily concerned with assisting the Government with raising resources. Such 'fiscal dominance' has its implications as well. No doubt the RBI has been taking corrective measures to neutralize the 'dominance' effects by discounting the system of automatic monetisation of budget deficit and indirectly trying to fix a limit on Central Government borrowings through the Ways and Means Advances (WMA). However, it cannot be denied that the constraints on fiscal policy front had impinged on the efficient conduct on monetary policy.

Enacting a Fiscal Responsibility Act can be one of the methods to attain fiscal stability. Reduction in fiscal deficit through a time-bound plan, supported by legislation has been followed in USA and New Zealand. It needs to be noted that fiscal responsibility is not the same thing as placing a ceiling on Government borrowings, although both are related. In this context, the experience of New Zealand can be instructive. In the early 80s, New Zealand's economy faced severe economic difficulties. After a prolonged period of high inflation (touching 10%), price and wage freeze were imposed. Control of all interest rates and lending was also widespread and the economy had large fiscal deficit which was financed by a mix of Central bank credit, compulsory Government stock purchase by financial institutions and foreign borrowing. A new government, in 1984, tried to address the problem by first devaluing the currency by 20% and lifting all curbs on financial sector. Through the new Reserve Bank of New Zealand Act 1989, the Central Bank was provided autonomy to pursue monetary policy through a unique system of Policy Targets Agreement between the Minister of Finance and the Governor of the RBN. Under this agreement, the Central Bank was provided with the mandate of targeting inflation between 0 to 2 per cent annually and any breach of these limits could lead to the dismissal of the Governor.

As part of structural reforms, the Government of New Zealand brought about corporatization and privatization culminating in the Fiscal Responsibility Act of 1994. While giving a long term perspective to fiscal management, pursuit of sound fiscal policies was ensured through law. One of the guiding principles of the Act was to ensure attainment of prudent levels of Crown debt and till it is attained, total operating expenses of the Government was to be lower than total operating revenues every year. Though the Act does not prescribe quantitative fiscal targets, it introduced a framework for setting fiscal objectives, monitoring progress in achievement thereof and bringing about transparency in Government finances. That the reform efforts have been successful is evident from the fact that New Zealand achieved fiscal surplus since 1994.

Although, adoption of similar legislation is desirable in the Indian context, certain issues need to be addressed. Given the past experience, deficit reduction will call for political will rather than law. However, moving towards a sound fiscal policy framework through law can facilitate easier political support to the moves on expenditure control by the government. Another issue can be to ensure the supremacy of the Parliament or Legislature in fiscal management while at the same time providing for flexibility. For instance, the Fiscal Responsibility Act of New Zealand provides that the Government may deviate from the Principles of the Act temporarily with justification and with assurance that they will return to them within a definite time-frame. A further issue could be whether to quantify the fiscal target or adopt a non-qualified approach. While New Zealand has successfully followed the second approach, USA adopted the quantification process. The enactment of Gramm-Rudman-Holdings (GRH) Act in 1985 aimed to balance the US budget and provided for a process of sequestration whereby if the targeted deficit is likely to be exceeded, fund would be automatically cancelled from domestic and defence related programmes. After several slip-ups, the US Government was able to bring about the first budget surplus in 1998. Given our federal nature, a question would also arise whether the fiscal responsibility act should cover only the Central Government or also states. Since the Act will call for transparency, the current secrecy in the budget process may have to be given up. Besides, enacting such legislation will also involve issues in granting autonomy to the Central Bank to pursue the goal of price stability.

> As India integrates further with the world economy, pursuing sound fiscal policies to ensure macro-economic stability and stable growth will gain in importance. Reform process can not be single track. Along with reforms in the trade and financial sectors, reforms in the fiscal front have to be pursued so that the goals of allocational efficiency and stable economic growth are achieved. Enacting Fiscal Responsibility Act could well be a right step in the right direction.[1]

Besides above, management of non-plan expenditure, unproductive expenditure, compacting administration and economic activities, better tax collection efforts, efficiency and sincerity of public sector undertakings are the necessary steps which should be taken.

---

1. Punjab National Bank, *Monthly Review*, February 2000, pp. 61-63.

5

STATE GOVERNMENT FINANCES IN GUJARAT

—B.M. Jani

State Government finances administration has drawn attention of economists, administrators and planners all over India. Since the 1980s, State Government finances in Indian economy have been found under heavy stress as most of the State Governments are facing a worsening budgetary situation which has substantially affected their development expenditure. This has happened largely due to declining share of tax and non-tax revenue in their budgets. Therefore, the second phase of financial sector reform has emphasised to manage budget deficits of State Government for sustainable period of time in general and during the years of 21st Century in particular. The States of India absorb large amount of Central budgetary funds from the federal Government and could not mobilize required financial resources. The economists have observed that during the years of the eighties, Central transfer to States on revenue account at 15.8% was higher than that of both Central revenue (14.5%) and states' own revenue (15%) and the same phenomenon has repeated during the years of the nineties. It has been visualised from budget documents that consolidated deficits of 25 States declined from 3.4% of GDP in 1990-91 to about 3.3% in 1991-92. However relative figures in rupees are higher. It appears that ability to manage large budget deficit of States has posed a new challenge after post economic reform period in India.

This paper aims at reviewing overall position of State Government finances in India in general and analysing State Government finances in Gujarat so as to offer policy options for the management of fiscal deficit at State level. For this, the present paper is divided into three parts: the first one reviews latest literature on the subject so as to sort out issues of debate, the second one expresses overview of State level situation in India, whereas, the third one examines a case of Government of Gujarat to manage budget deficits during the years of the nineties.

I

Retrospect

Serious effect is made by economists of research institutes and the Reserve Bank of India as well as academics to review State Government finances so as to prescribe resource mobilisation and management of budget deficits at State levels in India. However, policy options are not suited to all States uniformly considering nature of fiscal problems varies at each State level.

Govind Rao (1992)[1] made aggregate analysis of State finances in India so as to prescribe policy options after economic reform period. He has critically reviewed expenditure of State Governments which include salary of State employees, rising level of State subsidies, inefficient public sector enterprises, rising amount of debt payments to the centre, debt outstanding, etc. He suggested that in order to save expenditure of States about Rs. 7000 crore, he offered alternatives and sorted out areas of raising new resources by levying of proper fees in education at par of inflation level, rise in irrigation charges, fertiliser and electricity subsidies, other hidden subsidies to wipe out states' revenue deficits.

The Reserve Bank of India (1998)[2] has annually reviewed State Government finances in *RBI Bulletin* so as to know disparities of management of budget deficits loan account with the Centre by States. It has observed that States have not repaid principal and interest of loans of the Centre as revenue deficits of all States together increased from 1.1% of GDP in 1996-97 to 1.3 % in 1997-98. There are States like Tamil Nadu, Madhya Pradesh, West Bengal, Kerala and Andhra Pradesh having significant contribution of 85% of total of all States in India. Revenue deficit of 17 States ranges from Rs. 7696 crore in the case of Uttar Pradesh to Rs. 25 crore in the case of new State like Goa during the period, and cautioned State Governments to raise additional resources to bridge revenue deficits of states.

The report of Tenth Finance Commission (1997)[3] observed gloomy picture of States in spite of devolution of resources and transfer from the Centre to States and loan repayment problem of the Centre created a tension for states. The share of the States from the Centre has fallen in percentages and hence finance commission has periodically revised the formula of devolution of resources from tax revenue received from State levels. It is also a fact that the Centre has encroached in area of States to mobilise resources in the form of central excise and other levy.

The Government of Gujarat has periodically appointed expert committees to review State finances which include Raja Chelliah committee (1980)[4] and Sanat Mehta Committee (1994)[5]. It was a common voice of the committees that public expenditure is rising and new sources of funding are falling. However, committees suggested ways and means to raise resources at State level but most of them are not accepted and executed by the Government due to political reason.

Reddy (1996)[6] and Patel (1995)[7] examined performance of State Government finances with reference to budget in A.P. and Gujarat respectively. They have forcefully argued for mobilization of additional resources by State Governments and for political reason both the Centre and State could not do so. Even finance Ministers could not recover overdue amount of Income Tax from Ministers, MPs, MLAs and artists of film industry.

Similarly, Zath Nizar (1992)[8] Kripa Shankar (1998)[9] and Om Prakash (1999)[10] examined State Government finances with reference to Gujarat, Uttar Pradesh and Punjab during the years of nineties. They have examined tax and non-tax revenue in total revenue proceeds, rising amount of loan outstanding, etc.

Issues of Debate

1. It appears that State Governments are heavily relying upon the Centre and could not mobilise new resources from tax and non-tax sources.
2. Due to lack of State level reforms in pattern of public

finance State budget deficits have increased sizably in absolute amount but in percentages found stationary.

3. State subsidies have gone to relatively rich farmers who have benefited by planned agriculture sector investment but could not contribute to State governments. Cross-subsidization adversely affected State finances in general and rising budget deficits in particular.
4. The State Governments have used Central protection force during riots and communal harmonies in the case of border and non-border States which increased non-plan wasteful expenditure.
5. The State Governments could not increase land revenue and sales tax which are stagnant for the last many years and hence total revenue proceeds could not increase at desired level by states.
6. We do not have permanent finance commission to monitor State Government expenditure and there is no co-operation between State planning Board and Planning Commission, and Planning Commission with Finance Commission. Why do we not have public expenditure commission to monitor wasteful expenditure of both the Centre and State governments?
7. Internal public debt of States increased sizably and State could not repay loans received from the Centre. The RBI could not manage to monetise State budget deficits for different States of India.
8. Can Indian State learn lesson from Australian and USA federal Governments to manage State budgets for sustainable period of time?
9. Why State Governments could not introduce Value Added Tax system and rationalization of tax structure at State levels?

II

Aggregate Position of State Finances

Budget documents and RBI Bulletins reveal figures for State Governments. It appears that aggregate State Government finances created tension for the Centre for macro-economic management and to remove structural imbalances in the economy. Statistical relationship in linear regression equation between expenditure on goods and services and expenditure on wages and salaries do not show positive relationship during the years of the eighties and the years of nineties considering major high-income, middle-income states. This means expenditure on wages and salaries do not significantly contribute to administrative services, social services, economic services. Researches also maintained that India is becoming service economy as share of services increased notably to 49% in 1998 well above industry 30% of GDP.

It is also observed by Bureau of The Economic Times that State Governments could not increase average GDP above 5%. Gross fiscal deficits of States declined from 3.8% (GFD/GDP) in 1997-98. In the case of the Centre, it remained 5.2% during the year largely due to rise in non-plan and non-development expenditure by the centre. This means that the Centre has increased gross fiscal deficits than the states. Budget documents also reveal that in 1980-91 there was 42.3% share of the Central Government loans in State finances which increased to 48.7% in 1998-99 of total finances of State and the size of market borrowing increased from 5% to 12.9% during the period.

The Centre had to declare Rs. 3000 crore for ways and means assistance to address structural deficits of States for following programme :

(a) Reduction in non-plan revenue expenditure, through appropriate taxation and expenditure measures and down-sizing wherever possible,

(b) Pricing/subsidy reforms to reduce fiscal burden of the States and improve allocative efficiency,

(c) Institutional reforms, to improve regulation and efficiency in delivery of public services and

(d) Reduction in role of Government from non-essential areas, through decentralization, disinvestment and privatization.

Looking to sales tax laws and low proceeds of the tax, the Centre had to intervene for implementation of sales tax by all States and

Union Territories in November 1999. The RBI also relaxed FDI norms to raise investment at State levels.

A top level expert committee has been set up by the State Government in order to scale down the state's fiscal deficit by raising non-tax revenue which has reached to 6.1% of net State domestic product. The Government has also made an effort to scale down state's debt and planned to increase revenue. The policy document *Gujarat Infrastructure Agenda : Vision* 2010 predicts that fiscal deficit is about to reach 7.8% of Net State Domestic Product in 2001-2002 and outstanding debt is about to climb to Rs. 10,496 crore on March 2002. This will happen largely due to large committed capital expenditure by the State Government and revenue receipts lead to a deterioration of the financial position of State government.

The State Government also appointed State public finances reform committee under the chairmanship of Mr. Manu Shroff to look into ways and means to raise funds from different sources like an increase in fees of education, health services, charges of water supply for irrigation and private use. The committee is also going to recommend non-tax sources and imposition of fresh sources of tax so as to bridge revenue deficit of the government. However, the present year (2000-2001) proved most expensive due to large amount of expenditure incurred by the State to manage drought and semi-drought situation in many districts of Gujarat and transportation of water and hay in backward districts of the state. Very recently, the Finance Minister appealed in the parliament to follow recommendation of 11th Finance Commission's report to be submitted at the end of June 2000 but meanwhile parliament has approved a Bill to devolve 29% of tax to States from retrospective effect (from 1995).

The State Government has opened infrastructure investment for foreign players, foreign institutional players like American insurance companies so as to meet the target of capital outlay in infrastructure projects. Recently, Gujarat Industries and Investment Corporation made agreement for planned investment for about 70% of project costs of different needy projects. It is expected that remaining 30% cost will be born by banks and financial institutions. Aggregate investment in such projects include, Rs. 33,000 crore investment of which for power sector projects Rs. 14,183 crore, for ports Rs. 14,700 crore, Rs. 1013 crore for industrial township project, Rs. 850 crore for Infocity, and Rs. 2500 crore for gas grid across cities. It is decided that the State Government will provide 48% of total infrastructure investment though at a zero cost.

Similarly, there is a growing need to privatize loss-making State Government enterprises which require disinvestments by the Government and again compensation will have to be paid to the surplus or existing employees of closed or existing enterprises like Gujarat Textile Corporation, Gujarat Dairy Corporation and Gujarat Export Development Corporation, Gujarat State Transport Corporation and other enterprises. Huge investment is also required for power generation projects and construction of Express High ways in the state. Thus, the State will have to raise resources both for bridging revenue deficits and capital deficits in order to maintain rate of growth for sustainable period of time so as to manage Gujarat as number one State in industrial growth.

Action Plan by the State

1. It is most necessary for the State Government to make disinvestment in order to raise resources out of the budget in order to manage the budget deficit and to manage planned investment of the ninth five year plan period. These include loss making State enterprises as well as profit making enterprises also for better management and efficiency of the enterprises.
2. The State Government should allow private players for enterprises require special skill and cannot be managed by the Government bureaucrats. The State Government should not incur drought expenditure but hand it over to non-Government voluntary organization and it should be monitored by the different departments of the government. This exercise can stop malpractices observed by the political leaders in the management of drought expenditure.
3. There is a need for Public Expenditure Commission to

monitor and watch State Government expenditure as different ruling Government wastefully spent money from the treasury.

4. It is most necessary for the State Government to receive adequate share of salt cess, oil cess and other royalties for the units located in Gujarat which are managed by the Central Government enterprises. A Northern State has succeeded to do so.
5. The Government should execute recommendation of previous committees for State finances and raising of tax and non-tax revenue by the state. Now, there is no need for further committees.
6. The State Government and local self-Government should increase cost of public utilities like water, bus services, electricity charges to manage the budgets.
7. The State Government should stop all wasteful subsidies looking to rise in income of people and position of State finances.
8. The Central Bureau of Investigation should inquire about assets of political leader in the State irrespective of political affiliation and attempt to publish a list for recoverable amount of outstanding taxes from them.

REFERENCES

1. M. Govind Rao (1992) : *State level Budget Reforms : Some Proposals*, Indian Economic Association trust for Research and Development, New Delhi.
2. R.B.I. (1998) : *Reserve Bank of India Bulletin*, R.B.I. Mumbai, August.
3. Govt. of India (1994) : *The Report of the Tenth Finance Commission*, Ministry of Finance, Government of India, New Delhi.
4. Govt. of Gujarat (1980) : *The Report of Taxation Inquiry Commission* (Chaired by Raja Chelliah) Government of Gujarat, Gandhinagar.
5. *Ibid.* (1994) : *The Report of Gujarat State Finance Commission* (Chairman : Sanstbhai Mehta) Government of Gujarat, Gandhinagar.
6. I. Mahendra Reddy (1996) : *State Level Reform in India*, Presidential Address Andhra Pradesh Economic Association, Hyderabad.
7. Patel Himmatbhai (1995) : *Finances of Government of Gujarat*, Key Paper Gujarat Economic Association Silver Jubilee Conference Volume 26-27, January.
8. Zeth Nizar (1992) : "Gujarat State Finances" in Amlesh Bagchi, J.L. Bajaj and William Byred (ed.) *State Government in India*, Vikas Publishing House, New Delhi.

9. Kripa Shankar (1998) : "Uttar Pradesh Budget : 1998-99, State Finances in a shamble" *Economic and Political Weekly*, Vol. XXXIII, No. 42, November 14.

10. Om Prakash (1999) : State Finances in Punjab: Trends and Challenges in *Punjab Economy Emerging Issues*, Guru Nanak Dev University, Amritsar.

6

FINANCIAL STATUS OF ANDHRA PRADESH

—B. Satyanarayan and *C. Giri*

Andhra Pradesh with a population of 6.65 crore as per 1991 Census, is the fifth most populous State in the country. More than 70% of the State's population lives in villages. The State's population for 1999 is projected at 7.51 crores.

As per the advance estimates for the year 1999-2000, the Gross State Domestic Product at constant (1993-94) prices is estimated at Rs. 79268 crores. Likewise per capita income at constant (1993-94) prices for the year 1999-2000 is estimated at Rs. 9424.

A Draft 'Vision 2020 Document' was released on 26th, January 1999. It is the desire of the Government to make Andhra Pradesh State the foremost State in the Country in terms of growth, equity and quality of life. The basic thrust of the Vision Document is to make development totally sustainable. During the last four years, the State Government has launched several schemes. The Janmabhoomi programme embodies the principles of voluntarism, participation, transparency, accountability and promotes excellence in all walks of life. The quality and accessibility of primary education including the primary health care delivery systems have been substantially improved. Self help groups in many sectors have been actively promoted and expanded. The developmental effort of the Government has a special bias in favour of women and disadvantaged groups.

TABLE 1

Andhra Pradesh State's Gross Fixed Capital Formation for the Year 1991-92 to 1997-98

(Rs. in Lakhs)

Sr. No.	Sector	1990-91	1991-92	1992-93	1993-94	1994-95	1995-96	1996-97	1997-98
1.	Agriculture	66319	88894	93075	108232	116628	115671	119824	150267
2.	Forestry & Logging	2760	2690	3128	2287	2827	4683	7698	9890
3.	Fishing	3005	3503	4247	4749	3175	4979	7093	11004
4.	Mining & Quarrying	21950	19981	30815	28112	58295	28418	20243	21024
Primary Sector		94034	115068	131265	143380	180925	153751	154858	192185
5.	Manufacturing	173399	174317	215675	224824	401450	473687	591084	650151
6.	Construction	21711	42625	33298	26929	37735	36774	44729	88732
7.	Elect., Gas & Water Supply	58916	90269	64066	61375	115808	138162	131300	104325
Secondary Sector		254026	307211	313039	313128	554993	648623	767113	843208
8.	Transport, Storage & Communication	60178	43157	113366	131151	128281	144579	170799	194859
9.	Trade, Hotels & Restaurants	2489	2278	22166	22512	24307	35061	26605	13985
10.	Finance, Banking & Insurance	7700	14431	17500	21076	33422	54418	81045	120473
11.	Real Estate, Ownership of Dwellings and Business Services	110479	124651	143353	162438	175353	192904	202293	230688
12.	Public Administration	24616	31566	23985	35947	36480	37039	38124	47176
13.	Other Services	22802	21791	37429	52167	46263	46490	47142	47406
Tertiary Sector		228264	237874	357799	425291	444106	510491	566008	654587
Total		576324	660153	802103	881799	1180024	1312865	1487979	1689980

Gross Fixed Capital Formation

Capital formation assumes importance in the context of policy making by the State and Central Governments. It acts as an indicator in the measurement of economic growth of State. It reveals the potentiality of the investments in the public as well as the private sectors and gives net addition of the assets created during the year. Table 1 records data pertaining to Gross Fixed Capital Formation (GFCF) of A.P. from 1991-92 to 1997-98. It may be noted that the GFCF in Andhra Pradesh has gone up from Rs. 5763.24 crores in 1990-91 to Rs. 16899.80 crores in 1997-98, thereby recording a compound annual growth rate of 17.24%.

It is also a fact that GFCF of the A.P. State in 1996-97 was Rs. 14879.79 crores as against Rs. 327090 crores of All India GFCF. As per the provisional estimates the GFCF of A.P. State during 1997-98 stood at Rs. 16900 crores. The percentage change over previous year was 13.58.

The percentage change over previous year in GFCF in Andhra Pradesh and All India at current prices from 1990-91 to 1997-98 is recorded in table 2.

TABLE 2

Percentage Change over Previous Year in GFCF in A.P. and All India at Current Prices from 1990-91 to 1997-98

Sr. No.	Year	A.P.GFCF (Rs. in Crores)	% change over previous year	All India GFCF (Rs. in Crores)	% change over previous year
1.	1990-91	5763	30.34	124004	20.66
2.	1991-92	6602	14.55	136503	10.88
3.	1992-93	8021	21.50	158857	16.38
4.	1993-94	8812	9.86	183418*	9.97
5.	1994-95	11800	33.92	222459*	23.87
6.	1995-96	13129	11.26	290113*	25.50
7.	1996-97	14880	13.34	327090*	12.66
8.	1997-98	16900	13.58	357836*	9.40

Figures upto 1992-93 are based on series (base = 1980-81) and figures from 1993-94 onwards are based on new series (base = 1993-94).

It may be observed that the year-wise change in GFCF for the State of A.P. is consistently higher when compared to All India during all the years under study except 1995-96.

State Government's Expenditure

The total expenditure figures of the State Government (both Revenue and Capital) are recorded in table 3. It may be observed that the total State expenditure was hardly of the order of Rs. 117 crores in 1960-61, which was just 12% in the State Domestic Product. This has phenomenally increased to Rs. 23,764 crores in 1999-2000 which is nearly 30% of its State Domestic Product. The quinquennial figures are shown in table 3.

TABLE 3

State Domestic Product and Total Expenditure of the Government of A.P. at Current Prices

(Rs. in Crores)

Year	State Domestic Product of A.P.	Total Expenditure (Revenue + Capital) of A.P.	% of total expenditure to SDP
1960-61	983	117	11.90
1965-66	1521	228	15.00
1970-71	2523	328	12.98
1975-76	4218	673	15.96
1980-81	7209	1409	19.54
1985-86	12879	3159	24.52
1993-94	58227	10541	18.10
1994-95	61491	12459	20.30
1995-96	64966	14301	22.00
1996-97	69188	16265	23.50
1997-98	68105(P)	17745	26.10
1998-99	75530 (P)	21050	27.90
1999-2000	79268(E)	23764	30.00

Source : *CMIE*, March 2000

Note

(i) The figures from 1960-61 to 1985-86 denote Net State Domestic Product, while figures from 1993-94 to 1999-2000 stand for Gross Domestic Product. Hence, there will be some variation. But, this is unavoidable.

(ii) P stands for Provisional, while E stands for estimate.

The Government's overall expenditure has escalated to greater heights because it has undertaken a number of social and economic welfare schemes during the last 5-6 years. Some of the important schemes are shown below :

(i) State Population Policy Programme.

(ii) Chief Minister's Empowerment of Youth Programme (CMEY).

(iii) SC, ST and OBC Welfare Schemes including Hostels.

(iv) A Comprehensive programme for Economic & Social Development of the Scheduled Caste Families (Mundadugu) schemes.

(v) Minorities Welfare Scheme.

(vi) Tribal Welfare Scheme; A Development Scheme for Tribal Families (Chaitanyam) Scheme.

(vii) Housing and Habitat Improvement Programme.

(viii) Poverty Alleviation Programmes.

(ix) Drought Prone Area Programme (DPAP), Water Shed Area Programmes, Desert Development Programme (DDP), Integrated Wasteland Development Programes (IWDP).

Besides these, quite a number of other schemes have been started for the overall improvement of rural and urban areas. Hence the total expenditure is on the higher side.

State Government's Budget

Table 4 gives a total picture of A.P. Government's overall budgetary position. It shows both Revenue and Capital Accounts, thereby one can have an idea as to how the financial position is taking shape through time as far as A.P. is concerned.

The main components of current receipts are tax revenue, income from property households, grants and contributions. Total current receipts of the A.P. State Government has increased from Rs. 8250 crores in 1993-94 to Rs. 17,795 crore in 1999-2000 (Budget Estimates). Contrary to this, the receipts under capital account have shown a continuous declining trend from Rs. 21,656 crores in 1993-94 to Rs. 702 crores in 1999-2000, which is a serious matter to be reckoned with.

As far as State Expenditure is concerned, the main items under current account are: Salaries and Wages, Pensions and other Governmental Consumption including transfer payments to the rest of the economy. This has increased from Rs. 8018 crores in 1993-94 to Rs. 22,695 crores in 1999-2000, resulting in a deficit of Rs. 4900 crores during 1999-2000. As regards disbursements (expenditure) under Capital Account, it has risen from a low level of Rs. 2200 crores in 1993-94 to Rs. 7124 crores in 1999-2000. Capital transfers are the payments made to assist capital formation in other sectors of the economy such as Local Bodies, Corporations and Private Institutions.

TABLE 4

Budgetary Position of Andhra Pradesh

(Rs. in Crores)

S. No.	Item	1993 -94	1994 -95	1995 -96	1997 -98	1998 -99	1999 2000
I.	Revenue Account						
	(a) Revenue	8250	8583	10174	13200	15029	17795
	(b) Expenditure	8018	9322	10888	16177	19279	22695
	(c) Surplus (+) or Deficit (-)	232	-739	-714	-2977	-4250	-4900
II.	Capital Account						
	(a) Receipts	21656	5700	6551	549	502	702
	(b) Disbursements	22001	4965	5774	6106	6157	7124
	(c) Surplus (+) or Deficit (-)	-345	735	777	-5557	-5655	-6422
III.	Overall Surplus (+) or Deficit (-)	-113	-4	63	-8534	-9905	-11322

Source : Director of Economics & Statistics, Government of Andhra Pradesh, Hyderabad-4.

The overall deficit (Current and Capital Accounts) put together has been continuously rising from a low level of Rs. 112 crores in 1993-94 to as high as Rs. 11322 crores in 1999-2000, except the year 1995-96, wherein there is a surplus of Rs. 63 crores.

Most of the State Budgets would be always in the red unless they take hard decisions both in raising their revenues and also regulating their expenditure. Some suggestions are given below :

(i) Subsidy payments are either to be removed or atleast minimised, such as rice scheme being followed in A.P.

(ii) A sort of uniform tariff/pricing structure is to be followed or self-imposed in the areas of electricity, water, property tax, motor vehicle tax, etc.

REFERENCES

1. Gautam Mathur, "Basic Choices in Development," *Indian and Foreign Review*, 1, July 1972 (New Delhi).
2. Anil De, *Planned Industrialisation : An Approach to a Positive Strategy — Policy and Programme for India*, Hyderabad, (1968).
3. National Council of Applied Economic Research (NCAER), *Techno-Economic Survey of Andhra Pradesh*, New Delhi (1962).
4. Nadkarni, A.G., *Development Potential of Andhra Pradesh*, *Yojana*, May 17, 1970.
5. *Economic Surveys*, GOI, 1997-98 and 1998-99.
6. *Economic Surveys*, Government of Andhra Pradesh, 1997-98 and 1999-2000 (Finance and Planning), Planning Wing, Department.
7. *Economic Trends in Andhra Pradesh*, February 1989.
8. *Economic-cum-Functional Classification of the Budgetary Transactions*, Govt. of A.P., February 1999, Directorate of Economics and Statistics, Hyderabad-4.
9. B. Satyanarayan, *Development Potential of Andhra Pradesh*, *Yojana*, May 17, 1970.
10. ——, "Telangana Development : Problems and Possibilities;" *Indian Journal of Regional Science*, Vol. V, No. 2, 1973.
11. ——, (Co-Editor), *State Finances in India*, Delta Publishing House; Hyderabad-80 (2000).

7

RESTRUCTURING STATE FINANCES IN PUNJAB

—*Om Parkash, D.S. Dhingra* and *Navjot Raikhy*

The Union Government in India initiated a process of structural adjustment popularly known as economic reforms in order to correct distortions and weaknesses of earlier economic policies followed in the country. These economic reforms included de-licensing, changes in policies regarding foreign investment, trade, exchange rate, industry, fiscal affairs, etc. Although these economic reforms relate to different areas of the economy, yet it was expected that reforms would pave the way for all-round prosperity of the economy. However, things have turned out differently indicating the ineptness of our reform process. Fiscal management at the Central Government level has become an uphill task during recent years because of political instability, populist policies, fiscal indiscipline and low tax collections.[1]

The fiscal situation in the States appears more vulnerable if we take a look at the State finances. Now the focus of reforms has shifted from Centre to States in their second stage. The tasks before the States are very complex because we are dealing with reforms in delivery of services — quantitatively and qualitatively as also appropriate pricing or subsidies.[2]

Addressing the sixth meeting of the Inter-State Council (ISC) on May 20, 2000, the Prime Minister urged the States to reduce the growing subsidy in power, transport and other service sectors to improve their financial condition and help the country tide over the widening fiscal deficit. The combined fiscal deficit of the Centre and States amounted to almost 10 per cent of the Gross

Domestic Product (GDP) in 1999-2000 (R.E.). In other words the Governments of the Centre and the States combined are borrowing resources amounting a 10th of the national income.[3] This fiscal deficit was higher than the 1990 level when the country faced a severe balance of payment crisis.[4] The Prime Minister further said that many States feel that a solution lay in greater provision of funds by the centre. But he urged that they should realise that providing additional funds cannot solve the problem. The financial position of the Centre is itself strained.[5] The Chairman of the Eleventh Finance Commission, Prof. A.M. Khusro also voiced his concern regarding fiscal deficit and deteriorating financial position of both the Centre and states. He pointed out that the fiscal deficit of the Centre and the States have nearly doubled from 3.3 per cent and 2.1 per cent of GDP respectively in 1970-71 to 5.6 per cent and 4 per cent respectively in 1999-2000. This is reflection of the overshooting expenditure especially on account of increased outgo due to pay revision, pension and interest payments. He further said that revenue deficit as per cent of fiscal deficit for all States in 1999-2000 was estimated at 56.86 per cent as compared to 25.66 per cent in 1990-91, which is indicative of the fact that the larger part of borrowings were utilised for consumption purposes.[6] In view of the deteriorating financial position of the states, the Central Government had asked the Eleventh Finance Commission to draw up a monitorable fiscal reforms programme for reducing revenue deficit of the States and also recommend the manner in which the non-plan revenue grants should be linked to the progress in implementation of the programme.[7] It has been maintained that the initiated reforms at the national level for achieving the desired rates of growth cannot be a success unless they percolate at the State level. This is necessary because the State Governments account for 56 per cent and 85 per cent of the combined expenditure of the Centre and the States on social and economic services respectively.[8] The States account for about 53 per cent of the total expenditure of the Centre and States combined.[9] Thus, the present situation in the country demands a concerted effort by the Centre and States which may provide a new fillip to the ongoing reform process.

In the light of the above discussion, it is proposed to review the fiscal health of Punjab State during the period of economic reforms. The paper provides some suggestions by which the State Government may bring about restructuring of its public finances for restoring budgetary balance for economic stability.

The State's annual budget which reflects the composition of State's finances may be divided under two major heads, *i.e.,* Revenue Account and Capital Account of the budget.

Table 1 shows the financial position of Punjab Government since 1991-92.

The 'Revenue Account' deals with the proceeds of taxation and other receipts classed as Revenue and Expenditure therefrom.

The State has been under fiscal stress since 1984-85, when it became a 'Revenue Deficit State' from a 'Revenue Surplus State.'[10] It is observed from table 1 that the revenue receipts have increased from Rs. 3715.84 crore in 1991-92 to Rs. 10,585.18 crore (BE) in 2000-2001 giving an increase of 2.85 times. On the other hand, revenue expenditure increased to Rs. 13071.56 crore in 2000-2001 from Rs. 4196.71 crore in 1991-92, depicting an increase of 3.11 times. It shows the revenue expenditure has outpaced its revenue receipts during the period under study. It may further be observed from the Table that the entire period of study suffered from revenue deficit. The revenue deficit which was Rs. 480.87 crore in 1991-92 increased to Rs. 3104.35 crore in 1999-2000 (R.E.). It is estimated to be Rs. 2486.38 crore for the fiscal 2000-2001. The revenue deficit as a percentage of revenue receipts was 12.94 per cent in 1991-92. This ratio was 37.03 per cent in 1999-2000 (R.E.) and it is estimated to be 23.49 per cent for the fiscal 2000-2001. The revenue deficit as a percentage of Gross State Domestic Product (GSDP) was 2.10 per cent in 1991-92, it was 4.56 per cent in 1998-1999. During this year, the revenue receipts were 10 per cent of GSDP as compared to 14.56 per cent for revenue expenditure of the State Government. This indicates the deteriorating position of revenue account of the budgets of the State. An orthodox principle of fiscal management suggests that revenue expenditure which is basically a consumption expenditure should be fully met from revenue

TABLE 1

Financial Position of Punjab Government

(Rs. in Crore)

Item	1991-92	1992-93	1993-94	1994-95	1995-96	1996-97	1997-98	1998-99	1999-00 (RE)	2000-01 (BE)
Revenue Receipts	3715.84	2786.93	3276.63	5300.92	5184.75	5568.61	6351.30	5755.96	8382.56	10585.18
Revenue Expenditure	4196.71	3422.52	4043.56	6042.76	5634.99	6925.67	7835.20	8384.29	11486.91	13071.56
Revenue Surplus/ Deficit	-480.87	-635.59	-766.93	-741.84	-450.24	-357.06	-1483.90	-628.33	3104.35	-2486.38
Capital Account Receipts	1174.97	4312.51	1696.11	2059.07	1816.42	2295.00	2946.14	9925.49	11186.99	10925.36
Capital Account Disbursements	815.68	785.05	1177.16	1462.48	1368.66	621.64	1636.34	7168.57	8525.05	8550.95
Capital Account Surplus/Deficit	359.29	3527.46	518.95	596.59	447.76	1673.36	1309.80	2756.92	2661.94	2374.41
Overall Budgetary Balance	-121.58	2891.27	-247.98	-145.25	-2.48	316.30	-174.10	128.60	526.60	112.51

Source : Annual Financial Statement and Explanatory Memorandum on the Budgets of Government of Punjab (Various Issues).

receipts. In fact, an even more conservative principle of budgeting is to generate revenue surplus for capital expenditure *i.e.,* for creation of durable assets or extinguishing future liabilities.[11]

The 'Capital Account' is the account of expenditure incurred with the objective either of increasing concrete assets of a material character or of reducing recurring liabilities, such as those for future pensions by payment of capitalized value. It also includes receipts arising generally from sale of concrete assets intended to be applied as a set off to capital expenditure. Normally capital expenditure is met from borrowed funds and other sources outside the revenue account. Thus, it is logical to utilize capital receipts for investment expenditure. Table 1 further illustrates that there has been a surplus on capital account of the budgets of the State Government throughout the period under review indicating that the borrowed funds have been utilized for meeting the revenue deficit of the State. The surplus on capital account was Rs. 359.29 crore in 1991-92, which grew to Rs. 2661.94 crore in 1999-2000 (B.E.). It is expected to be Rs. 2374.41 crore during the fiscal 2000-2001 (B.E.).

The overall worsening situation of the State Government relevant for financial investment expenditure is illustrated in table 2.

TABLE 2

Revenue Deficit/Gross Fiscal Deficit in Punjab *vis-a-vis* All States

(Percentage)

Year	Revenue Deficit/Gross Fiscal Deficit	
	Punjab	All States
1985-90	9.9	7.7
1990-95	45.9	24.6
1996-97	92.65	43.25
1997-98	59.89	37.10
1998-99	55.34	53.80
1999-00	71.05	55.38

Source : Reserve Bank of India, Finances of State Governments : 1997-98 S-21 and CMIE, Public Finance in India 1999-2000.

Table 2 shows that revenue deficit as proportion of fiscal deficit has risen considerably in Punjab. It has risen from 9.9 per cent during the period 1985-90 to 71.05 per cent in 1999-2000. It was as high as 92.65 per cent in fiscal 1996-97. It may further be observed from the table that this ratio was quite higher in Punjab as compared to all states. This has resulted in a situation where the borrowings by the States are now being devoted more and more to the financing of revenue expenditures. This is likely to lead to further worsening of the fiscal situation in future. The resources available for investment will decline in the foreseeable future unless this trend is reversed.

The overall worsening fiscal situation of the State Government is further illustrated in table 3.

TABLE 3

Selected Fiscal Ratios for Punjab State *vis-a-vis* All States

Year	Capital Outlay/Gross Fiscal Deficit		Interest Payments/Revenue Expenditure	
	Punjab	All States	Punjab	All States
1985-90	21.0	62.4	12.1	10.8
1990-95	27.3	55.3	16.0	13.6
1996-97	31.3	45.9	22.9	15.3
1997-98	32.0	49.2	27.1	16.2

Source : Reserve Bank of India, finances of State Governments : 1997-98, February 1998.

Table 3 illustrates that capital outlays as a proportion of gross fiscal deficit has increased from 21 per cent in 1985-90 to 32 per cent in 1997-98. But this ratio is quite low when compared to all states. Though capital outlay as a proportion of fiscal deficit has declined for all States during the period under study but still it is far above than the ratio of Punjab State. With regard to interest payments as a proportion of revenue expenditure it may be stated that these have increased from about 12 per cent in 1985-90 to 27 per cent in 1997-98, giving an increase of 2.24 times. This ratio is also far above as compared to all states. The ratio for all States has increased from about 11 per cent to 16 per cent, depicting an increase of 1.5 times.

Having examined the deteriorating broad contours of the budgets of Punjab State, it would now be useful to examine the structure of revenue receipts of the State.

Table 4 shows the structure of revenue receipts in Punjab. The Table highlights that State's own tax revenue increased from Rs. 1542.96 crore in 1991-92 to Rs. 4204.65 crore in 1999-2000 and these are expected to grow to Rs. 5350.45 crore in 2000-01. The revenue from State's own tax revenue has shown a growth of 3.47 times during the period under consideration. Its share in the revenue receipts has varied between 41.52 per cent in 1991-92 to 65.60 per cent in 1993-94. During the fiscal 1999-2000, its share was about 50 per cent of total revenue receipts and is expected to be around 50 per cent during fiscal 2000-01. State's own non-tax revenue has ranged between 11.79 per cent in 1992-93 to 44.29 per cent in 1991-92. It share is expected to be 34.54 per cent during fiscal 2000-01. Its growth works out to be 2.22 times during the period under review. On the other hand, State's share in Central taxes has shown a growth of 2.29 times and the grants from the Centre showed a rise of 3.88 times during the period of study. The share of Central taxes was 7.89 per cent in the total revenue of the State Government. It was around 10 per cent during the fiscal 1997-98 and 1998-99. The year 1999-2000 and 2000-01 showed a decline in share of Central taxes. These are expected to contribute 6.34 per cent in 2000-01. The share of grants from Central Government was 6.29 per cent in 1991-92 and is expected to be 8.57 per cent for the fiscal 2000-01. Thus, on the whole, it may be stated that State's own revenues accounted for more than 80 per cent during the fiscal 1999-2000 and are expected to contribute about 85 per cent during the fiscal 2000-01.

It may be stressed here that the share of Central taxes is determined constitutionally on the recommendations of Finance Commission. The formula used for horizontal allocation gives more weight to equity and the progressive States like Punjab lose because of higher per capita income and other developmental indicators.

It is observed from Table 5 that the two taxes, *viz.* sales tax and States excise duty, are the dominant taxes in the revenue of

TABLE 4

Structure of Revenue Receipts in Punjab

Item	1991-92		1992-93		1993-94		1994-95		1995-96	
	Rs. Crore	%age	Rs. Crore	%age	Rs. Crore	%age	Rs. Crore	%age	Rs.Crore	%age
State's own tax revenue	1542.96	41.52	1758.75	63.11	2149.64	65.60	2599.64	49.04	2650.99	51.13
State's Share in Central Taxes	293.27	7.89	349.01	12.52	378.80	11.56	424.33	8.00	441.78	8.52
Total Tax Revenue	1836.23	49.44	2107.76	75.63	2528.44	77.16	3023.97	57.04	3092.77	59.65
State's Own Non-Tax Revenue	1645.72	44.29	328.75	11.80	414.06	12.64	2003.62	37.80	1777.37	34.28
Grants from the Centre	233.90	6.29	350.41	12.57	334.13	10.20	273.91	5.17	314.61	6.07
Total Non-tax Revenue	1879.62	50.58	679.16	24.37	748.19	22.84	2277.53	42.97	2091.98	40.35
Total Revenue Receipts	3715.85	100	2786.92	100	3276.63	100	5301.50	100	5184.75	100

Table 4 (*Contd.*)

Items	1996-97		1997-98		1998-99		1999-00		2000-01	
	Rs. Crore	%age	Rs. Crore	%age	Rs. Crore	%age	Rs. Crore	%age	Rs. Crore	%age
State's own tax revenue	2734.66	49.11	3044.67	47.94	3262.47	56.68	4202.65	50.14	5350.45	50.55
State's Share in Central Taxes	528.35	9.49	456.98	10.34	587.16	10.20	671.11	8.01	671.11	6.34
Total Tax Revenue	3263.01	58.60	3501.65	58.28	3849.63	66.88	4873.76	58.14	6021.56	56.89
State's Own Non-Tax Revenue	1944.80	34.92	2356.53	37.10	1507.35	26.19	2540.83	30.31	3655.99	34.54
Grants from the Centre	360.80	6.48	29.12	4.62	398.65	6.93	967.96	11.55	907.63	8.57
Total Non-tax Revenue	2305.60	41.40	2385.65	41.72	1906.00	33.12	3508.79	41.86	4563.62	43.11
Total Revenue Receipts	5568.61	100	5887.30	100	5755.63	100	8382.56	100	10585.18	100

Source : Same as table 1.

TABLE 5

Share of Major Components of State's Own Tax Revenue

Item	1991-92		1992-93		1993-94		1994-95		1995-96	
	Rs. Crore	%age	Rs. Crore	%age	Rs. Crore	%age	Rs. Crore	%age	Rs.Crore	%age
Land Revenue	3.5	0.23	3.65	0.21	2.9	0.13	3.87	0.15	3.2	0.12
Stamps and Registration	119.47	7.74	143.5	8.16	173.63	8.08	245.57	9.45	227.52	8.58
Sales Tax	752.71	48.78	807.67	45.92	961.19	44.71	1195.59	46.00	1183.41	44.64
State Excise	479.64	31.09	592.78	33.70	766.13	35.64	883.41	33.99	943.61	35.59
Tax on Vehicles	121.14	7.85	138.31	7.86	166.36	7.74	178.1	6.85	190.65	7.19
Tax and Duties on Electricity	60.55	3.92	66.34	3.77	73.04	3.40	87.27	3.36	92.87	3.50
Other Taxes and Duties	0.52	0.03	0.45	0.03	6.4	0.30	1.78	0.07	9.73	0.37
State's Own Tax Revenue	1542.96	100	1758.75	100	2149.64	100	2599.06	100	2650.99	100

Table 5 *(Contd.)*

Item	1996-97		1997-98		1998-99		1999-00		2000-01	
	Rs. Crore	%age	Rs. Crore	%age	Rs. Crore	%age	Rs. Crore	%age	Rs.Crore	%age
Land Revenue	3.02	0.11	3.57	0.12	2.9	0.09	1.25	0.03	2.75	0.05
Stamps and Registration	182.44	6.67	233.83	7.68	258.12	7.68	350	8.33	450	8.41
Sales Tax	1264.5	46.24	1401.14	46.02	1489.66	44.30	2100	49.97	3000	56.07
State Excise	1000.72	36.59	1143.7	37.56	1204.27	35.82	1300.8	30.95	1385.8	25.90
Tax on Vehicles	195.23	7.14	215.68	7.08	266.72	7.932	305	7.26	350	6.54
Tax and Duties on Electricity	79.92	2.92	37.79	1.24	31.9	0.95	136	3.24	152.3	2.85
Other Taxes and Duties	3.29	0.12	3.15	0.10	8.9	0.26	9.6	0.23	9.6	0.18
State's Own Tax Revenue	2734.66	100	3044.67	100	3362.47	100	4202.65	100	5350.45	100

Source : Same as table 1.

the State Government. These two taxes combined together contributed about 80 per cent in 1991-92 and are expected to provide 82 per cent in the fiscal 2000-01. The proceeds from sales tax have increased from Rs. 752.71 crore in 1991-92 to Rs. 2100 crore in 1999-2000 (R.E.), giving an increase of 2.79 times. These are expected to yield Rs. 3,000 crore during the fiscal 2000-01. It has been pointed out that while sales tax accounts for about 60 per cent or more of the tax revenue of most of the states, its share is as low as 40 per cent in Punjab. This is despite the fact that Punjab has one of the highest per capita consumption expenditure.[12] Further, it may be mentioned here that more than 50 per cent of the sales tax revenue accrues from food items and inputs used in further production of goods. This raises the question of incidence of tax (probably regressive) and substantial 'cascading' that it would be causing.[13] Further, it may be observed that there is a structural shift in the economy of Punjab State. As the share of agriculture falls with overall development there is every hope that revenue of the State will increase. This is because agriculture is by and large untaxed. In fact the share of agriculture in GDP has fallen from 33.76 per cent in 1980-81 to 26.52 per cent in 1998-99. Correspondingly the share of secondary sector increased from 20.01 per cent to 24.48 per cent and that of manufacturing sector from 11.66 per cent to 16.60 per cent. The share of services sector (tertiary) has also increased from 30.86 in 1980-81 to 34.45 per cent in 1998-99. Hence, there is every likelihood that the contribution of sales tax in GDP will rise in future. This can be achieved by imposing Value Added Tax (VAT) on the sales of both goods and services. Levying such a tax requires consensus among the States and an amendment in the constitution. Keeping in view the setting up of Constitutional Review Commission, this problem can be solved for bringing buoyancy in sales tax revenue.

As regards the state's excise duty it may be mentioned here that it is a restrictive duty, Its objective is to control trade and consumption of spirits and other intoxicants. A welfare State is not expected to allow this great social evil to grow simply in the interest of revenue. It may be pointed out here that on theoretical grounds it is possible to make out a powerful case for the enforcement of the policy of prohibition, but on economic grounds it is very difficult to follow such a policy. This is because the State is suffering from financial difficulties at the present junctures.

It may be noted that during 1999-2000 (RE) about three-forth of the total excise duties accrued from country made spirits which are generally consumed by the poor. Thus, this duty may be defended as a deterrent tax but not a tax for revenue. But in practice, it is treated as a tax for revenue because generally increase in revenue is the objective of excise policy.

The other major components of State's own tax revenue are stamps and registration, taxes on motor vehicles and electricity duty. In case of stamps and registration, it has been mentioned that a major factor adversely affecting the revenue productivity in all States is considerable under reporting of sale values and cosequent substantial tax evasion.[14] Thus, there is a need for rationalisation of stamps and registration fee in view of rising prices and value of property. Moreover, converting of specific rates into ad valorem rates would improve the revenue productivity from this source.

The growth of revenue from taxes on vehicles depends upon increase in the number of vehicles. It may be referred here that vehicle density per square kilometer in Punjab is the highest among states. Keeping this in view, the State Government by restructuring and rationalizing this tax can generate more revenue. The share of electricity duty in the State revenue depends upon the consumption of electricity especially of industrial sector in the State. As the share of manufacturing sector in the State is increasing, there is a possibility of increasing its share. The other taxes like entertainment tax and land revenue have lost significance in the structure of taxation in Punjab.

Finally, it may be stated that the populist measures practiced by the successive Government in the State have adversely affected the revenue of the State. Here, mention may be made of provision of free electricity to the agricultural sector, the provision of free irrigation to the farmer and abolition of land revenue in the State.

Non-Tax Revenue of Punjab State

The principal components of State's own non-tax revenue are interest receipts, dividends and profits, user charges from economic services, social services and other general services. Table 6 exhibits that there has been a wide variation in the interest receipts as a percentage of total non-tax revenue. Interest receipts accounted for 87.73 per cent of total non-tax receipts in 1991-92. This ratio has declined to 6.96 per cent in 1998-99 and the estimated ratio for the fiscal 2000-2001 is 16.96 per cent. Here, it may be noted that the States where public sector units run efficiently and commercially profitably, they are in a position to contribute significant amounts to the State public exchequer in exchange the form of interest and dividends. Gujarat, Maharashtra and Tamil Nadu can be referred as examples in this regard. The State Government can increase its revenue from this source by putting its departmental undertaking more on commercial lines.[15]

General services include the receipts from police, jails, stationery and printing, public works, other administrative services, contributions and recoveries towards pension and other retirement benefits and miscellaneous general services. The share of general services in the total non-tax receipts was only 2.72 per cent in 1991-92 but it increased to 78.46 per cent in 1995-96 and is estimated to provide 69.29 per cent of total non-tax revenue of the State in 2000-2001.

The contribution of social services in the total non-tax revenue which includes receipts from education, medical and public health, water supply and sanitation, social security and welfare, etc. was only 2.02 per cent in 1991-92. It was 3.38 per cent during the fiscal 1998-99 and is estimated to be 2.15 per cent for the fiscal 2000-2001. The major contribution under this head is from education, medical and public health which account for about one-half of the total receipts from this head. The receipts from water supply and sanitation contribute about one-forth of this category of non-tax revenue.

Most of the non-tax revenues in the category of economic services are derived from road transport, major and medium irrigation projects, forestry and wild life, crop husbandry, animal

TABLE 6

Composition of Non-Tax Revenue

Item	1991-92		1992-93		1993-94		1994-95		1995-96	
	Rs. Crore	%age	Rs. Crore	%age	Rs. Crore	%age	Rs. Crore	%age	Rs.Crore	%age
Interest Receipts	1443.84	87.73	71.3	21.69	74.00	17.87	81.54	4.07	87.05	4.90
Dividends and Profits	0.54	0.03	5.59	1.70	3.14	0.76	7.85	0.39	4.61	0.26
General Services	44.81	2.72	56.73	17.26	67.54	16.31	1607.66	80.24	1394.57	78.46
Social Services	33.25	2.02	35.49	10.80	45.64	11.02	50.08	2.50	39.18	2.20
Economic Services from which :	123.21	7.49	159.6	48.55	223.74	54.03	256.49	12.80	251.96	14.18
a) Major and Medium Irrigation	15.11	0.92	15.8	4.81	16.41	3.96	16.91	0.84	17.16	0.97
b) Road Transport	88.19	5.36	100.86	30.68	156.14	37.71	176.26	8.80	176.97	9.96
c) Forestry and Wild Life	3.29	0.20	3.89	1.18	5.28	1.28	5.15	0.26	6.89	0.39
Total Non-Tax Revenue	1645.72	100	328.75	100	414.06	100	2003.62	100	1777.37	100

Table 6 *(Contd.)*

Item	1996-97		1997-98		1998-99		1999-00		2000-01	
	Rs. Crore	%age	Rs. Crore	%age	Rs. Crore	%age	Rs. Crore	%age	Rs. Crore	%age
Interest Receipts	1464.14	75.28	982.84	41.70	104.86	6.96	617.02	24.28	620.33	16.97
Dividends and Profits	5.43	0.28	2.99	0.13	1.49	0.10	9.14	0.36	2.78	0.08
General Services	167.17	8.60	1052.87	44.68	1069.28	70.94	1553.2	61.13	2533.34	69.29
Social Services	52.25	2.69	52.37	2.22	51.03	3.39	72.39	2.85	78.65	2.15
Economic Services from which :	255.81	13.15	265.46	11.26	280.69	18.62	289.08	11.38	420.89	11.51
a) Major and Medium Irrigation	16.94	0.87	19	0.80	16.28	1.08	9.9	0.39	15.62	0.43
b) Road Transport	175.34	9.01	187.7	7.97	214.72	14.24	229.32	9.03	347.17	9.50
c) Forestry and Wild Life	5.31	0.27	7.66	0.33	6.52	0.43	7.2	0.28	7.9	0.22
Total Non-Tax Revenue	1944.8	100	2356.53	100	1507.35	100	2540.83 3	100	3655.99	100

Source : Same as table 1.

husbandry and co-operation. It is evident from the table that the share of economic services in the total non-tax revenue was 7.49 per cent in 1991-92 which increased abruptly to 48.54 per cent in 1992-93 and further increased to 54.03 per cent in 1993-94. This increase was by and large due to increase in revenue from road transport during these years. Its share again declined to 12.8 per cent in 1994-95 and was around 11 per cent in 1999-2000. The estimated share of economic services in the total non-tax revenue for the fiscal 2000-2001 is 11.5 per cent. It may be noted here that out of the estimated 11.5 per cent share of economic services, about 9.5 per cent would be contributed by road transport, 0.42 per cent by major and medium irrigation and about 0.2 per cent by forestry and wild life. It may be mentioned here that finances of state's irrigation department were deep in red even before the provision of free irrigation to farmers in 1997. The revenue loss to the State Government is estimated to be Rs. 32 crore due to the provision of free supply of irrigation. It has been observed that the public has got used to not paying adequately for these services. It is perceived that the services are provided by the Government and therefore do not have to be paid for. Second, with the quality of service being poor, the public is loath to pay higher charges. For breaking this vicious circle, there is a need for the imposition of higher user charges accompanied by palpable improvements in the quality of service. The attainment of higher efficiency in the provision of service can progressively lead to lower charges.[16]

Moreover, targeted price subsidies should be provided where better off users pay fully the cost of service and the poor have access at the subsidised price.

Development and Non-Development Expenditure on Revenue Account

Table 7 shows the growth and composition of revenue expenditure into developmental and non-developmental heads. It is evident from the table that the total revenue expenditure of the Government increased from Rs. 4196.75 crore in 1991-92 to Rs. 13,071.56 crore for the fiscal 2000-01 (BE), giving an increase of 3.11 times. The development expenditure as a proportion of

TABLE 7

Development and Non-Development Expenditure in Punjab

Item	1991-92		1992-93		1993-94		1994-95		1995-96	
	Rs. Crore	%age	Rs. Crore	%age	Rs. Crore	%age	Rs. Crore	%age	Rs. Crore	%age
Development Expenditure	3183.44	75.85	1936.73	56.59	2111.09	52.21	2192.69	36.29	2552.94	45.30
a) Social Services	955.87	22.78	1029.53	30.08	1146.87	28.36	1231.54	20.38	1590.91	28.23
b) Economic Services	2227.57	53.08	907.2	26.51	964.87	23.86	961.15	15.91	962.03	17.07
Non-Development Expenditure of which :	981.94	23.40	1452.65	42.44	1875.35	46.38	3802.34	62.92	3017.66	53.55
a) Interest Payment and Servicing of Debt	360.59	8.59	410.61	12.00	1042.17	25.77	1243.69	20.58	1489.59	26.43
b) Administrative Services	404.31	9.63	812.30	23.73	547.08	13.53	668.73	11.07	6670.68	11.90
c) Pension and Misc. General Services	146.3	3.47	159.81	4.67	198.18	4.90	1760.45	29.13	724.83	12.86
Transfers to Local Bodies	31.33	0.75	33.14	0.97	57.12	1.41	47.73	0.79	64.39	1.14
Total Expenditure on R/A	4196.75	100	3422.52	100	4043.56	100	6042.76	100	5633.99	100

Table 7 (*Contd.*)

Item	1996-97		1997-98		1998-99		1999-00		2000-01	
	Rs. Crore	%age	Rs. Crore	%age	Rs. Crore	%age	Rs. Crore	%age	Rs. Crore	%age
Development Expenditure	3947.15	56.99	4121.83	52.60	3919.63	46.75	5903.65	51.40	5980.18	45.75
a) Social Services	1639.22	23.67	2062.16	26.31	2639.54	31.48	3487.31	30.36	3541.58	27.09
b) Economic Services	2307.93	33.32	2059.67	26.29	1280.09	15.27	2416.34	21.04	2438.60	18.66
Non-Development Expenditure of which :	2911.91	42.05	3713.37	47.39	4464.66	53.25	5583.26	48.61	7091.38	54.25
a) Interest Payment and Servicing of Debt	1634.44	23.60	1848.76	23.60	2316.34	27.62	2474.71	21.54	2931.21	22.42
b) Administrative Services	776.42	11.21	963.45	12.30	1095.97	13.07	1184.53	10.31	1319.35	10.09
c) Pension and Misc. General Services	351.85	5.08	659.58	8.42	727.14	8.67	1561.97	13.60	2577.62	19.72
Transfers to Local Bodies	66.61	0.96	70.30	0.90	73.30	0.87	88.61	0.77	0.40	0.003
Total Expenditure on R/A	6925.67	100	7835.20	100	8384.29	100	11486.91	100	13071.56	100

Source : Same as table 1.

Gross State Domestic Product was 13.95 per cent in 1991-92 which declined to 6.86 per cent in 1998-99. The development expenditure is comprised of the expenditure on social services like education, health, housing etc. and economic services like agriculture, industry, transport, energy, etc. The former may be viewed upon as an investment in human development and the latter in physical capital development. The development expenditure rose from Rs. 3183.44 crore in 1991-92 to Rs. 5980.18 crore in 2000-2001 (BE), giving an increase of 1.88 times. Its share in the total revenue expenditure declined substantially during the period of study. Its share was 78.85 per cent in 1991-92, which declined to 51.39 per cent in 1999-2000 (RE). Its estimated share for the fiscal 2000-01 is 45.75 per cent. The expenditure on social services showed an increase of 3.7 times, whereas the growth in expenditure on economic services was 1.09 times. The share of social services was about 30 per cent in 1999-2000 (RE) and is estimated to be 27.09 per cent for the fiscal 2000-01 (BE). In social sectors, education has been getting higher priority than health sector over the years. The strategy of spending more on education rather than health has been suggested on the ground that apart from direct benefits, the external benefits of education in terms of reduction in morbidity rate, mortality rate and birth rate are quite substantial and hence a rupee spent on education ultimately gives higher returns than that on health.[17] On the other hand, the share of economic services was 21.04 per cent for the year 1999-2000 (RE) and the estimated share for the fiscal 2000-01 is 18.66 per cent. Similarly, it has been mentioned that Punjab's share of development expenditure (Revenue and Capital expenditure) in the total expenditure was 58 per cent in 1996-97. This ratio was the lowest among the high income States in India. The low development expenditure share is partly because of the very large interest burden on account of expenditure incurred on fighting terrorism in the State.[18]

On the other hand, the non-developmental expenditure increased from Rs. 981.94 crore in 1991-92 to Rs. 7091.38 crore for the fiscal 2000-01, giving an increase of 7.22 times. The share of non-development expenditure was 23.4 per cent in 1991-92, which increased to 48.6 per cent in 1999-2000 (RE). The estimated share of non-development expenditure in the total revenue expenditure of the State is 54.25 per cent for the fiscal 2000-01 (BE). The non-development expenditure as a percentage of GSDP rose from 4.30 per cent in 1991-92 to 7.75 per cent in 1998-99.

The table further reveals that the share of interest payments and servicing of debt in the total revenue expenditure was 8.59 per cent in 1991-92, which increased to 21.54 per cent in 1999-2000 (RE) and is estimated to be 22.42 per cent for the fiscal 2000-01. Interest payments and servicing of debt alone accounted for 44.32 per cent of non-development expenditure on Revenue Account in 1999-2000 (RE) and is estimated to be 41.76 per cent for the fiscal 2000-01 (BE). The mounting debt obligations are caused by the willful fiscal indiscipline by successive Governments to depend upon public borrowing rather than tax collection to meet their expenditure needs.[19] The total outstanding debt for the year 1998-99 (RE) was Rs. 24202.97 crore. Here, it may be pointed out that a sizable amount of loan was in the form of special term loan for combating insurgency and militancy in the State which is national problem. Now, this loan has been waived by the Government of India on the recommendations of Eleventh Finance Commission.

The administrative expenditure rose to Rs. 1319.35 crore in 2000-01 (BE) from Rs. 404.31 crore in 1991-92, giving an increase of 3.26 times. Its share in the total expenditure was 9.63 per cent in 1991-92, which increased to 13.07 per cent in 1998-99. The estimated expenditure on administrative services for the fiscal 2000-01 is 10.09 per cent. The main reason in the rise of administrative expenditure may be due to the implementation of the recommendations of the Fourth Pay Commission.[20] The expenditure on pension and miscellaneous general services has increased from 3.48 per cent in 1991-92 to 13.59 per cent in 1999-2000 (RE) and is estimated to be 19.71 per cent for the fiscal 2000-01 (BE). The pension and other retirement benefits account for 13.04 per cent of the total non-development expenditure on Revenue Account for the fiscal 2000-01 (BE).

Concluding Comments

The State's finances have been under stress since 1984-85, when Punjab became a 'Revenue Deficit' State from a 'Revenue Surplus' State. There have been persistent deficits on revenue account during the period under consideration. The revenue deficits as a percentage of revenue receipts was 12.94 per cent during the year 1991-92. The ratio was 37.03 per cent in 1999-2000 (RE) and is estimated to be 23.49 per cent for the fiscal 2000-01. The revenue deficit as a percentage of Gross State Domestic Product was 2.10 per cent during 1991-92 which increased to 4.56 per cent in 1998-99. This indicates the deteriorating position of the revenue account part of the budget in the State.

The steady deterioration in the revenue account of the budgets in the State has resulted in enlargement of State's Gross Fiscal Deficit leading to large scale borrowings. The curtailment of Gross Fiscal Deficit could be achieved through deceleration of capital expenditure, which would, however, have adverse implications for growth. The improvement in Gross Fiscal Deficit, therefore, be achieved through revenue account. This requires a restoration of semblance of balance between revenue receipts and revenue expenditure. The State Government would have to ensure that its revenue expenditure does not grow at a higher rate as compared to its revenue receipts. For this purpose, there is an urgent need to contain Government's expenditure especially non-plan non-development part of public expenditure in the State. The present study has revealed that State's non-development expenditure has shown a galloping growth at the cost of development expenditure. This tendency of growing non-developmental expenditure needs to be reversed. This is required urgently in the State at present because there must be massive effort to improve social infrastructure and straighten physical infrastructure to the levels where it can attract the private capital investment in the State.

The increase in non-development expenditure is due to committed expenditure on interest payments and administrative expenditure on salaries and pensions. The problem of subsidies needs immediate attention. Here the emphasis should be squarely on implicit subsidies, which deprive the State of scarce resources.

Further, an increase in user charges would substantially reduce pressure on fiscal deficit. This is because augmentation of revenue through non-tax sources like user charges would result in higher revenue and efficiency gains. It would provide the much needed resources for investment in social and infrastructural sectors.

The populist policies followed by the successive State Governments due to political expediency have brought financial crunch in the State. The free supply of power to the agricultural sector, provision of free irrigation to the farmers and abolition of land revenue need to be reviewed and it may be examined. 'Do these really help the deserving?'

Moreover, the limit to dependence on financial resources from the Union Government are recognised now and the State has to restructure and rationalise it own tax revenue for ensuring better tax collection.

There is a great scope for increasing tax through sales tax administration in the State because the structure of the State's economy is changing in favour of its secondary and tertiary sectors.

In addition to the above suggestions, the State Government may introduce zero-Base Budgeting in some selected departments so that those programmes which have outlived their utility are eliminated or allocation of funds to these are restricted.

Finally, it is expected from the State Government that by taking appropriate steps it would bring the State's finances out of the present dismal state of affairs.

REFERENCES

1. Mishra, R.K., "Restructuring State Finances in Andhra Pradesh," *Arthavijnana*, Vol. XLI, No. 3, September 1999, p. 217.
2. Reddy, Y.V., "State Finances and RBI Initiatives," *Reserve Bank of India Bulletin*, April 1998, p. 360.
3. Rekesh Mohan, "Fiscal Correction for Economic Growth," *Economic and Political Weekly*, Vol. XXXV, No. 24, June 10, 2000, p. 2034.
4. *The Hindustan Times*, Vol. LXXVI, No. 139, May 21, 2000, p. 1.
5. *The Sunday Tribune*, Vol. 120, No. 139, May 21, 2000, p. 1.
6. *The Tribune*, Vol. 120, No. 141, May 23, 2000, p. 12.
7. *Ibid.* p. 15.

8. Rangarajan, C., "Finances of State Governments-Highlights," *RBI bulletin*, October 1993, pp. 307-64.
9. Aggarwal, M.R., "New Economic Policies, Growth and Reforms at the State Levels (Case of Punjab)" in Bawa R.S. and Raikhy P.S., *Punjab Economy : Emerging Issues*, Guru Nanak Dev University, Amritsar, p. 464.
10. Government of Punjab, *Economic Survey of Punjab*, 1999-2000. Economic Advisor to Punjab Government, Chandigarh, p. 92.
11. Ganguli, S.P., *Control over Public Expenditure*, Concept Publishing Company, New Delhi, 1997, p. 42.
12. Om Parkash, "State Finances in Punjab — Trends and Challenges." *Punjab Economy : Emerging Issues* (Editors : R.S. Bawa and P.S. Raikhy), Guru Nanak Dev University, Amritsar, p. 375.
13. Kurian, N.J., "State Government Finances — A Survey of Recent Trends," *Economic and Political Weekly*, Vol. XXXIV, No. 19, May 8, 1999.
14. Guhan B., "State Finances in Tamil Nadu," in Amresh Bagchi, J.L. Bajaj and William A. Byred (ed.), *State Finances in India*, Vikas Publishing House Pvt. Ltd., New Delhi, 1992, pp. 240-41. Also see Ramalingom, Aiyer R. and Kurup, K.N., "State Finances in Kerala" in the same Volume, p. 442.
15. Kurian, N.J., *op. cit.*, p. 1121.
16. Rakesh Mohan, *op. cit.*, p. 2035.
17. Dholkia, Archna R., "Changes in The Trend and Structure of Fiscal Expenditure in Gujarat," *Anvesak*, Vol. 28, No. 1, January-June 1998, p. 21.
18. Gill, Sucha Singh, "Fiscal Crisis in Punjab," *The Tribune*, November 11, 1997, p. 8
19. Aggarwal, M.R. *op. cit.*, p. 467.
20. Government of Punjab, *op. cit.*, p. 92.

8

FINANCIAL MANAGEMENT OF HARYANA GOVERNMENT SINCE 1967-68

—*Chandra Ballabh Sharma*

The economic performance of any Government depends in a significant degree upon the management of its finances, *i.e.,* how it taps its sources of revenue and how it utilizes these. To generate adequate finances and to put these to proper use in accordance with a certain well-thought-out strategy for socio-economic development of the economy is indeed a major responsibility of the Government. Sound financial management is the key to success in this context. As Porwal (1971) has aptly said : "Sound finances depend upon sound Government and sound Government depends upon sound finances."

In order to perform its function — social, economic and general — Government needs funds which have to be garnered from a variety of sources. For instance, these may be collected from the public in the form of taxes and non-taxes. When funds thus collected fall short of the expenditure targets, the Government takes recourse to public debt to bridge the gap between its income and expenditure. In the present paper, an attempt has been made to study the financial management of Haryana Government in terms of the behaviour of its revenues, expenditures, and public debt during the period of 1967-68 to 1998-99 and to draw implications of analytical and policy relevance.

BUDGETARY POSITION

It is important in this context, first, to analyse the dynamics of the budgetary position of Haryana Government in terms of revenue account and capital account.

Revenue Account

Revenue Account shows the comparative picture of the current income and current expenditure. The difference indicates a surplus, deficit, or balance depending on whether income exceeds, falls short of, or equals the expenditure. The dynamics of the revenue account of the State is depicted in tables 1 and 2. It can be seen that Haryana experienced a surplus in this account during the first twenty one years and a deficit during the last eleven years of the period under study. The revenue surplus was as high as Rs. 162.82 crores in 1986-87 and as low as Rs. 4.61 crores in 1969-70. The revenue deficit was the lowest in 1992-93, being Rs. 1.71 crores, and the highest in 1998-99, being Rs. 1135.60 crores (Budget Estimate).

Capital Account

Capital Account gives the comparative statement of the borrowings and investments of the Government. Capital receipts are of capital nature which cannot be applied as a set-off to capital expenditure. Capital expenditure deals with the expenditure usually met from borrowed funds with the main objective of increasing capital assets. The dynamics of the capital account of Haryana Government is also depicted in tables 1 and 2. It is shown that during the first 18 years, from 1967-68 to 1984-85, there has consistently been a deficit. Thereafter, wide fluctuations — at times surplus and at other times deficit — have characterised this account.

The overall budgetary position of the State Government includes transactions on both revenue and capital accounts. So far as overall account in Haryana is concerned, there have been wide fluctuations over the period under study. For instance, in 1967-68, there has been an overall deficit but in 1968-69 and 1969-70 there were surpluses. Thereafter, there have been deficits, surpluses without any consistent pattern. However, overall behaviour shows surplus in 15 years and deficit during the other 17 years.

TABLE 1

Tax And Non-Tax Revenue of Haryana Government

(Rs. in Crore)

Year	State's Own Tax Revenue	Share in Central Taxes	Total Tax Revenue	State's Own Non-Tax Revenue	Grant-in-aid from Central Govt.	Total Non-Tax Revenue	Total Revenue
1967-68	26.34	7.20	33.55	21.95	6.26	28.22	61.77
1968-69	34.72	8.74	43.46	28.56	6.59	35.15	78.81
1969-70	37.70	10.15	47.85	29.66	7.44	37.09	84.95
1970-71	43.89	12.28	56.16	33.49	9.52	43.00	99.18
1971-72	51.10	13.32	64.42	38.39	12.17	50.63	114.91
1972-73	60.49	17.73	78.23	44.00	15.15	59.14	137.38
1973-74	73.51	19.01	92.52	43.56	17.30	60.86	153.38
1974-75	99.11	20.77	119.88	55.15	12.08	67.23	187.11
1975-76	116.96	27.13	114.09	64.75	19.69	84.44	228.53
1976-77	138.07	19.58	157.65	78.16	21.98	100.14	257.79
1977-78	147.68	37.58	185.26	78.46	32.12	110.58	295.84
1978-79	170.58	33.06	203.64	93.38	37.81	131.19	334.83
1979-80	197.30	54.06	251.36	111.78	38.98	150.76	402.12
1980-81	233.91	61.23	295.14	119.30	45.49	164.79	459.93
1981-82	290.61	68.04	358.65	137.99	39.43	177.42	536.07
1982-83	336.68	72.60	409.28	159.88	42.46	202.34	611.62
1983-84	365.88	80.77	446.65	179.54	72.40	251.94	698.59
1984-85	405.40	93.55	498.65	214.47	77.02	291.49	790.44
1985-86	501.71	85.51	587.22	258.12	115.00	373.12	960.34
1986-87	565.85	97.21	663.06	296.63	170.49	467.12	1130.18
1987-88	664.39	107.52	771.91	378.00	153.93	531.93	1303.84
1988-89	795.42	120.61	916.03	354.71	170.34	525.05	1441.08
1989-90	910.12	154.11	1064.23	445.93	97.08	543.01	1607.24
1990-91	1069.54	185.90	1255.44	511.10	146.88	657.98	1913.42
1991-92	1300.20	219.45	1519.65	546.09	176.04	722.13	2241.78
1992-93	1446.87	261.94	1708.81	460.27	208.55	668.82	2377.63
1993-94	1588.91	282.45	1871.36	1340.55	269.54	1610.09	3481.45
1994-95	1887.85	317.14	2204.99	3473.42	204.00	3677.42	5883.41
1995-96	2168.96	360.47	2529.43	2186.81	298.49	2485.30	5014.73
1996-97	2143.12	431.87	2575.01	3132.67	340.65	3473.37	6048.33
1997-98	2413.42	531.00	2944.42	2230.18	542.20	2772.38	5716.80
1998-99	3584.13	614.60	4198.73	1644.73	661.23	2305.96	6504.69

Source : *Statistical Abstract of Haryana*, Various Issues.

TABLE 2

Development and Non-Development Revenue and Capital Expenditure of Haryana Government

(Rs. in Crore)

Year	Devlop. Revenue Expend.	Non-dev. Revenue Expend.	Total Revenue Expend.	Dev. Capital Expend.	Non-Dev. Capital Expend.	Total Capital Expend.	Total Expendi--iture	Revenue Surplus(+) Deficit(-)
1967-68	-	-	55.53	-	-	9.39	64.92	6.24(+)
1968-69	-	-	67.70	-	-	6.66	74.36	11.11(+)
1969-70	-	-	80.34	-	-	5.33	85.67	4.61(+)
1970-71	-	-	93.39	-	-	24.87	118.26	5.79(+)
1971-72	-	-	107.07	-	-	44.34	151.41	7.84(+)
1972-73	-	-	117.04	-	-	25.44	142.48	20.34(+)
1973-74	91.27	44.07	135.34	29.36	0.56	29.92	165.26	18.04(+)
1974-75	118.02	46.77	164.79	25.46	0.39	25.85	190.64	22.32(+)
1975-76	131.55	55.45	187.00	38.24	1.24	39.48	226.48	41.53(+)
1976-77	152.35	56.92	209.27	66.28	2.24	68.52	277.79	48.52(+)
1977-78	174.51	56.54	231.05	48.59	1.83	50.42	281.47	64.79(+)
1978-79	205.62	76.00	281.62	78.80	1.64	80.44	262.06	53.21(+)
1979-80	249.03	68.77	317.80	106.22	1.45	107.67	425.47	84.32(+)
1980-81	302.27	98.45	400.72	99.97	2.29	102.26	502.98	59.21(+)
1981-82	364.31	121.23	485.54	110.48	2.76	113.24	598.78	50.53(+)
1982-83	425.11	141.75	566.86	152.67	2.99	155.66	722.52	44.76(+)
1983-84	469.18	153.56	622.74	109.00	2.97	111.97	734.71	75.85(+)
1984-85	561.27	199.60	760.87	155.08	3.14	158.22	919.09	29.57(+)
1985-86	615.79	238.43	854.22	197.29	4.43	201.72	1055.94	106.12(+)
1986-87	675.54	291.82	997.36	167.16	5.10	172.26	1139.62	162.82(+)
1987-88	929.30	358.18	1287.48	56.84	3.65	60.49	1347.97	16.36(+)
1988-89	1026.65	416.28	1442.93	135.79	4.36	140.15	1583.08	1.85(-)
1989-90	1148.98	552.75	1701.73	129.45	3.22	132.67	1834.40	94.49(-)
1990-91	1295.68	637.39	1933.07	179.17	6.99	186.16	2119.23	19.65(-)
1991-92	1500.30	773.72	2274.02	138.46	7.53	145.99	2420.01	32.24(-)
1992-93	1621.49	757.85	2379.34	222.71	5.62	228.33	2607.67	1.71(-)
1993-94	1751.27	1649.73	3401.00	296.08	6.84	302.92	3703.92	80.45(+)
1994-95	2781.49	3491.43	6272.92	200.34	6.24	206.58	6479.50	389.51(-)
1995-96	2787.24	2574.32	5361.56	277.66	8.21	285.87	5647.43	346.83(-)
1996-97	3092.09	3674.91	6767.00	428.94	17.71	446.65	7213.65	718.67(-)
1997-98	3495.16	2852.93	6348.09	474.31	10.34	484.65	6832.74	631.29(-)
1998-99	4674.49	2965.80	7640.29	1107.76	41.93	1149.69	8789.98	1135.60(-)

Source : *Statistical Abstract of Haryana*, Various Issues.

TABLE 3

Tax and Non-Tax Revenue of Haryana Government

(Percentages)

Year	State's own Tax Revenue	Share in Central Taxes	Total Tax Revenue	State's Own Tax Revenue	Grants-in-aid from Central Govt.	Total Non-Tax Revenue	Total Revenue
1967-68	43	11	54	36	10	46	100
1968-69	44	11	55	36	9	45	100
1969-70	44	12	56	35	9	44	100
1970-71	44	13	57	34	9	43	100
1971-72	44	12	56	33	11	44	100
1972-73	45	12	57	32	11	43	100
1973-74	48	12	60	28	12	40	100
1974-75	53	7	64	29	7	36	100
1975-76	51	12	63	28	9	37	100
1976-77	54	7	61	30	9	39	100
1977-78	49	14	63	27	10	37	100
1978-79	51	10	61	28	11	39	100
1979-80	49	13	63	28	9	37	100
1980-81	51	13	64	26	10	36	100
1981-82	54	13	67	26	7	33	100
1982-83	55	12	67	26	7	33	100
1983-84	52	12	64	26	10	36	100
1984-85	51	12	63	27	10	37	100
1985-86	52	9	61	27	12	39	100
1986-87	50	9	59	26	15	41	100
1987-88	51	8	59	29	12	41	100
1988-89	55	9	64	25	11	36	100
1989-90	57	9	66	28	6	34	100
1990-91	56	10	66	27	7	34	100
1991-92	58	10	68	24	8	32	100
1992-93	61	11	72	19	9	28	100
1993-94	46	8	54	39	7	46	100
1994-95	32	5	37	59	4	63	100
1995-96	43	7	50	44	6	50	100
1996-97	35	8	43	52	5	57	100
1997-98	42	10	52	39	9	48	100
1998-99	55	10	65	25	10	35	100

Source : table 1.

TABLE 4

Development and Non-Development Revenue and Capital Expenditure of Haryana Government

(Percentages)

Year	Revenue Expenditure	Capital Expenditure	Development Expenditure	Non-Development Expenditure
1967-68	86	14	-	-
1968-69	91	9	-	-
1969-70	94	6	-	-
1970-71	79	21	-	-
1971-72	71	29	-	-
1972-73	82	18	-	-
1973-74	82	18	73	27
1974-75	86	14	75	25
1975-76	83	17	75	25
1976-77	75	25	79	21
1977-78	82	18	79	21
1978-79	78	22	79	21
1979-80	75	25	83	17
1980-81	80	20	80	20
1981-82	81	19	79	21
1982-83	76	24	80	20
1983-84	85	15	79	21
1984-85	83	17	78	22
1985-86	81	19	77	23
1986-87	85	15	74	26
1987-88	96	4	73	27
1988-89	91	9	73	27
1989-90	93	7	70	30
1990-91	91	9	70	30
1991-92	94	6	68	32
1992-93	91	9	71	29
1993-94	92	8	55	45
1994-95	97	3	46	54
1995-96	95	5	54	46
1996-97	94	6	49	51
1997-98	93	7	58	42
1998-99	87	13	66	34

Source : table 2.

PUBLIC REVENUE

Total Revenue

Total revenue is the sum of total tax revenue and total non-tax revenue. While the total tax revenue includes (i) State's own tax revenue and (ii) Share in Central taxes, the total non-tax revenue is the sum of (i) State's own non-tax revenue and (ii) grants-in-aid from the Central Government.

The total revenue of the State Government in absolute terms was Rs. 16.77 crores in 1967-68 which increased to Rs. 6504.69 crores in 1998-99 showing a more than 100-fold increase over the 32 year period at current prices. Another significant point to note is that except for 1994-95 and 1996-97, tax revenue has been of greater relative importance than non-tax revenue as source of State's revenues. Taken together, State's own tax revenue and non-tax revenue are more than three times of receipts from the Central Government. On an average, less than 25 per cent of the total revenue is received from the Centre and more than 75 per cent is generated from own sources of State Government. Total revenue of Haryana Government increased at an annual compound growth rate of about 17 per cent at current prices.

Tax Revenue

Total tax revenue is defined as the sum of State's own tax revenue and its share of Central taxes. This was Rs. 33.55 crores in 1967-68 which increased to Rs. 4198.73 crores in 1998-99. In relative terms, total tax revenue as percentage of total revenue fluctuated between 50 per cent and 65 per cent. Tax revenue increased at an annual compound growth rate of about 17 per cent during the period under study. State's own tax revenue increased from Rs. 26.34 crores in 1967-68 to Rs. 3584.13 crores in 1998-99. Share in Central taxes was Rs. 7.20 crores in 1967-68 which increased to Rs. 614.60 crores in 1998-99. In relative terms, the share of Central taxes remained virtually the same, with minor fluctuations.

Non-Tax Revenue

Total non-tax revenue consists of State's own non-tax revenue and grants-in-aid from the Central Government. Central grants mean the transfer of resources from the Central Government to the State Governments to bridge up the gap between revenue and expenditure of the States. Grants are also given for some specific purposes such as meeting the natural calamities, etc. State's own non-tax revenue which was Rs. 21.95 crores in 1967-68 increased to Rs. 1644.73 crores in 1998-99, and grants-in-aid from the Centre increased from Rs. 6.26 crores to Rs. 661.23 cores during the same period. The proportionate share of grants-in-aid from the Central Government ranges between 4 per cent (1994-95) and 15 per cent (1986-87) with wide fluctuations. But, on an average, the Centre's proportionate share has gone down in relative importance here too. State has come to depend more and more on its own means in this context.

PUBLIC EXPENDITURE

Total Expenditure

Total expenditure here signifies the sum of total revenue expenditure and total capital expenditure incurred by the Government for various purposes. There has been a continuous increase in the total expenditure of Haryana Government over the period under study from Rs. 64.92 crores in 1967-68 to Rs. 8789.98 crores in 1998-99, showing an overall increase of about 130 times over the 32-year period and an annual compound growth rate of about 17 per cent. This shows that the State Government has been making ever-growing expenditure for various purposes, partly developmental and partly non-developmental.

Revenue Expenditure

Revenue expenditure consists of development and non-development revenue expenditure. In 1967-68, total revenue expenditure of Haryana Government was Rs. 55.33 crores which increased to Rs. 7640.29 crores in 1998-99. Thus, like total expenditure, revenue expenditure has also increased by about 130 times. Its annual compound growth rate has been about 18 per cent at current prices. Its relative share in total expenditure is much greater than that of the capital expenditure. The proportion of revenue expenditure in total expenditure has been as high as 97 per cent in 1994-95.

Capital Expenditure

Capital expenditure also has two components — development and non-development expenditures. But it is mostly developmental, and the non-developmental capital expenditure is rather non-significant. Capital expenditure in the State increased from Rs. 9.39 crores in 1967-68 to Rs. 1149.69 crores in 1998-99. But the increase has not been a steady one. It has shown wide fluctuations along the time path. Relative share of capital expenditure in total expenditure has ranged between 15 per cent and 25 per cent upto 1987-88. Thereafter it has been less than 9 per cent of the total expenditure. It is important to note that although capital expenditure as a proportion of total expenditure has shown a declining trend, yet, in absolute terms, it has increased at an annual compound growth rate of about 12 per cent over the period under study.

Development and Non-Development Expenditure

Total expenditure of the State Government has been divided into following major components :

1. Expenditure on Social and Community Development
2. Expenditure on Economic Services
3. Expenditure on General Services

Expenditure on social and community services includes expenditure on education, art and culture, health and family welfare, housing, labour and employment, social security and welfare, etc. Expenditure on economic services includes expenditure on agricultural and allied services, industry and minerals, water and power development, transport and communication, etc. Expenditure on general services includes expenditure on administrative services, fiscal services, interest payment and debt servicing and organs of State.

The first two categories of expenditure constitute the development expenditure while the third category is non-development expenditure. Expenditure on economic services has been comparatively higher than the expenditure on social and community development. In 1973-74, expenditure on social and community development was Rs. 39.87 crores which increased to Rs. 1784.45 crores in 1998-99. On the other hand, expenditure on economic services was Rs. 80.76 crores in 1973-74 and Rs. 3125.86 crores in 1998-99.

In proportionate terms, development expenditure was 73 per cent of total expenditure in 1973-74 and 83 per cent in 1979-80. But, thereafter it has shown a declining trend to 66 per cent in 1998-99. This shows that, on the whole, the relative share of development expenditure has been on the decline.

The expenditure on general services, which is a non-development expenditure, was Rs. 44.63 crores in 1967-68. It increased to Rs. 3007.73 crores in 1998-99. In relative terms, it was 27 per cent of total expenditure in 1973-74 which declined to 17 per cent in 1979-80, but thereafter it has been showing an increasing trend, which cannot be considered healthy as it indicates declining relative importance of developmental expenditure and, therefore, needs to be checked.

Expenditure on Debt Servicing and Interest Payment

Expenditure on debt servicing and interest payment increased from Rs. 13.28 crores in 1967-68 to Rs. 997 crores in 1998-99, an increase of about 75 times in absolute terms over the period of 32 years. However, in relative terms, as a percentage of total expenditure, it has shown a declining trend, which is, in a sense, a positive indicator.

Public Debt

Public debt includes the internal debt of the State Government and loans and advances from the Central Government. The data on public debt receipts, disbursement and net are presented in table 5. Thus, public debt (receipts) of Haryana Government was Rs. 20.67 crores in 1967-68 which increased to Rs. 2398.77 crores in 1998-99, giving an annual compound growth rate of about 11 per cent over the period under study. While the internal debt created by the State Government was Rs. 65.49 crores in 1973-74 and Rs. 1153.91 crores in 1998-99, the amount of loans and advances received from the Centre has been Rs. 36.16 crores in 1973-74 and Rs. 1244.86 crores in 1998-99.

Disbursement of debt means redemption of debt. The gap between debt receipts and debt disbursement shows the net debt

TABLE 5

Loan Account of Haryana Government

(Rs. in Crore)

Year	Public Debt (Receipt)	Public Debt (Disbursement)	Public Debt (Net)	Servicing Interest Payment
1967-68	20.67	19.91	0.76	13.28
1968-69	45.89	38.11	7.78	15.23
1969-70	37.57	36.95	0.62	16.12
1970-71	63.30	41.75	21.55	15.99
1971-72	146.33	103.61	42.72	16.89
1972-73	143.01	115.99	27.02	19.93
1973-74	101.65	80.09	21.56	21.28
1974-75	103.57	84.34	19.23	20.58
1975-76	156.09	141.17	14.92	24.55
1976-77	125.92	114.49	11.43	24.59
1977-78	224.63	187.50	37.13	23.55
1978-79	172.34	123.70	48.64	40.74
1979-80	210.32	156.31	54.01	26.32
1980-81	296.39	230.70	65.69	41.51
1981-82	405.21	307.03	98.18	49.52
1982-83	525.37	432.35	93.02	55.07
1983-84	625.84	491.99	133.85	62.18
1984-85	677.00	538.49	138.51	82.97
1985-86	849.54	651.30	198.24	98.25
1986-87	542.78	354.95	147.83	132.62
1987-88	542.07	443.09	98.98	150.11
1988-89	444.93	257.80	187.13	160.55
1989-90	390.38	180.17	210.21	206.42
1990-91	591.97	296.33	295.64	242.03
1991-92	433.97	196.15	237.82	321.80
1992-93	418.92	163.47	255.45	365.07
1993-94	668.21	287.88	380.33	434.09
1994-95	636.96	235.67	401.29	486.94
1995-96	1072.08	248.46	823.62	555.73
1996-97	443.22	442.51	500.71	715.90
1997-98	1793.68	874.95	918.73	820.00
1998-99	2398.77	1056.95	1341.82	947.00

Source : *Statistical Abstract of Haryana*, Various Issues.

incurred during the period. In Haryana, disbursement of public debt has been less compared to receipts during the period under study. As a result, the net public debt has been increasing throughout this period. For instance, disbursement of public debt in 1973-74 was only Rs. 80.09 crores as against Rs. 101.65 crores of receipts in that year thereby leaving a gap of Rs. 21.56 crores as net public debt. By 1998-99, the net public debt had increased to a hefty Rs. 1341.82 crores.

THE BURDEN OF PUBLIC DEBT

Debt-Income Ratio

The debt-income ratio is a widely used indicator of strength and stability of the economy in relation to its debt. Mishra (1985) suggested that if the rate of increase in the State income approximately keeps pace with that of the growth of debt, there is apparently not much to worry. If the rate of increase in income is greater than the rate of increase in debt, the magnitude of burden can be said to have declined. But if the rate of increase in debt is greater than the rate of rise in income, the magnitude of debt service costs may be said to be increasing. These costs will restrict outlay for the current activities and, if they were too heavy, they may undermine the credit worthiness of the Government. The economy may face crisis resulting from a higher debt-income ratio. It is, therefore, important that the debt-income ratio is kept as low as possible either by restraining recource to debt burden or by promoting income generation, or by doing both together.

Table 6 shows the debt-income ratio of Haryana Government for the period from 1973-74 to 1998-99. As is evident from the Table, the debt-income ratio has been fluctuating widely. The public debt as a part of the Net State Domestic Product (NSDP) which was 8.07 per cent in 1973-74, increased to 10.72 per cent in 1977-78 and declined to 7.49 per cent in the following year (1978-79). But, thereafter, it continuously increased upto 1985-86 when it reached 14.68 per cent. However, it shows a declining trend during the following years and it was as low as 3.01 per cent in 1996-97. The figures for the last two years (1997-98 and

TABLE 6

Indicators of the Burden of Public Debt

(Percentages)

Year	Debt as % of NSDP	Interest Payment as % of NSDP	Interest Payment as % of Total Revenue	Interest Payment as % of Total Revenue Expenditure
1973-74	8.07	1.69	23.00	15.72
1974-75	7.26	1.44	17.17	12.49
1975-76	9.66	1.52	17.04	13.13
1976-77	6.62	1.29	15.60	11.75
1977-78	10.72	1.12	12.71	10.19
1978-79	7.49	1.77	20.00	14.47
1979-80	8.68	1.09	10.47	8.28
1980-81	9.78	1.37	14.06	10.36
1981-82	11.89	1.45	13.81	10.20
1982-83	13.50	1.41	13.46	9.71
1983-84	14.84	1.47	13.92	9.98
1984-85	14.55	1.78	16.63	10.90
1985-86	14.68	1.70	16.73	11.50
1986-87	8.93	2.18	20.00	13.71
1987-88	8.04	2.23	19.45	11.66
1988-89	4.44	1.60	17.53	11.13
1989-90	3.50	1.85	19.40	12.13
1990-91	4.34	1.77	19.28	12.52
1991-92	2.68	1.19	21.18	14.15
1992-93	2.29	2.00	21.36	15.34
1993-94	3.26	2.12	23.20	12.76
1994-95	2.60	1.99	22.08	7.76
1995-96	3.85	2.00	21.97	10.37
1996-97	3.01	2.28	27.80	10.58
1997-98	5.39	2.46	27.85	12.92
1998-99	6.25	2.60	23.75	13.05

1998-99) are budget estimates and cannot, therefore, be taken to reflect the final position.

Interest Payment on Debt and Income

It indicates the extent to which the income has to be taxed by the Government to enable it to obtain sufficient revenues for meeting the annual interest charges. If the income is high in relation to the interest payment, the Government can raise adequate revenues for this purpose without seriously increasing the burden on the tax payers. But the situation will be difficult if the interest charges are high in proportion to the income.

Table 6 shows the interest payment as percentage of NSDP. As is evident from the table, there are wide fluctuations in the behaviour of interest payment-income ratio. In 1973-74, it was 1.69 per cent which declined to 1.09 per cent in 1979-80 but thereafter it continuously increased upto 1987-88. With some fluctuations in the ensuing years, it rose in 1998-99. On the whole, one could say that the burden on this account is relatively less.

Debt Service and Tax Revenue

The financial burden of the debt requires allocation of tax revenue for meeting the debt servicing burden. The ratio of interest cost to tax revenue indicates the fiscal burden of the debt. We have, therefore, calculated the proportion of tax revenues needed to meet the interest payments and analysed the changes in the ratio of debt servicing costs to the total tax revenue to find out if the annual interest payments have increased faster than the tax revenue.

Tax revenue of the State Government shows an increasing trend from Rs. 33.55 crores in 1967-68 to Rs. 4198.73 crores in 1998-99. During the same period, interest payment increased from Rs. 13.28 crores to Rs. 997 crores. This ratio thus was 23 per cent in 1973-74 and was about the same in 1998-99, though in 1996-97 and 1997-98, the ratio did go up to as high as 27.80 per cent and 27.85 per cent respectively. But these figures are based on budget estimates and may not be treated as indicating a final position in this regard.

In terms of the rates of growth, we find that the growth rate of tax revenue has been greater than that of interest payment. In this sense, the fiscal burden on the State economy has actually been declining. This signifies that the conditions have been conductive to capital formation to the extent that tax revenues excess of debt-servicing were channelised into investment projects.

Public Expenditure and Interest Cost

The ratio of interest payment to public expenditure enables us to assess the extent to which the interest payment impinges upon the socially desirable public expenditure. Reserve Bank of India has been using this ratio as an indicator of the indebtedness of States in its analysis of the State finances.

Interest payment as percentage of total revenue expenditure of the State Government has been computed and presented in table 6. The Table shows that during the period under study, total revenue expenditure has been continuously increasing while interest payment at times increased and at times fell. But one thing is clear that the expenditure on revenue account increased at a faster rate than the interest payment. The ratio was 15.72 per cent in 1973-74 which declined in the following years and reached the minimum of 9.71 per cent in 1982-83. Thereafter, it fluctuated but remained at less than 15 per cent.

In conclusion, we can say that our analysis of the various parameters has shown that Haryana has been doing fairly well as regards its financial management. However, further follow-up in this direction is certainly called for to make more effective use of State finances for productive and income-generating purposes. Proper studies to select more productive investment projects should precede the final investment decisions to meet the aspirations of the people of the State in particular, and of the country, in general.

REFERENCES

Economic Survey of Haryana Government, Chandigarh, Various Issues.

Mishra, D.K., *Public Debt and Economic Development in India*, Print House, Lucknow, 1985.

Muni Lal, Haryana : *On High Road to Prosperity*, Vikas Publishing House, Delhi, 1974.

Porwal, L.S., *State Finances in India : A Case Study*, Sultan Chand and Sons, Delhi, 1971.

Statistical Abstract of Haryana, Chandigarh, Various Issues.

9

FISCAL SCENARIO IN HIMACHAL PRADESH

—*Meenakshi Sooden*

There has been a lot of discussion on the problem of fiscal imbalances of the Central government, but the issue at the State level has not received so much attention. State finances are no less important, because the States raise about 35 per cent of revenue and account for nearly 56.5 per cent of total combined budgeted total expenditure of the central, States and Union territories.[1] An in-depth study of State finances can help one to understand the problems and issues associated with raising and disbursement of funds by the State government. Analysis of State budgetary operations can also help one to understand the development issues of a state.

Himachal Pradesh being a hilly State with difficult geographical terrains has peculiar problems of development, and these natural hazards impinge upon its finances also. The analysis of finances carried out in other States is only of limited applicability in the context of Himachal Pradesh.

Though Himachal Pradesh on account of its huge financial liabilities and limited resources, was never a State which was financially healthy, yet the situation deteriorated at the end of 1980's, when the Central plan assistance, at the instance of Planning Commission was reduced further. In addition to it the definition of special category States was also modified by the

1. Ashok K. Lahiri, "Budget Deficits and Reforms," *Economic and Political Weekly*, Vol. XXXV, No. 46, Nov. 11, 2000, p. 4049.

Ninth Finance Commission leading to financial problems in the State.

Though in the past some studies dealing with finances of the State have been conduced, yet on account of policy changes at the Central level the financial position of the State has been considerably effected, compelling it to resort to huge borrowings. Thus, it is important that a fresh study of State finances in Himachal Pradesh is made.

In the present paper broad trends of State finances in Himachal Pradesh during the period 1981-82 to 1999-2000 are analysed. In the first section of the study both revenue and expenditure in the revenue account of the budget are analysed, and in the second section of the paper revenue and expenditure under the capital account of budget are discussed. In the third section of the study overall implications of emerging fiscal scenario, and required corrective measures are discussed in brief.

I

Revenue Receipts and Revenue Expenditure

The overall financial position of the State since 1981-82 is exhibited in table 1. The Table contains both the composition of receipts and expenditure in the State. Revenue receipts in the State went up from Rs. 234.21 crores in 1981-82 to Rs. 2510.58 crores in 1999-2000, at a linear growth rate of 14 per cent per annum. In 1981-82, revenue receipts were 86.12 per cent of total receipts, but particularly since 1994-95, because of fiscal crisis noticed in the State, reliance on borrowings increased. As a result in 1999-2000, they formed just 68.79 per cent of total receipts (table 2).

As far as the composition of revenue receipts is concerned, the share of the State's own receipts has continued to remain less than half of that of the Central transfers during the period under study. However, as far as the State's own revenue is concerned a major share is coming from tax revenue. Total tax revenue rose from Rs. 38.61 crores in 1981-82 to Rs. 666.52 crores in 1999-2000, registering a linear growth rate of 17.11 per cent per annum. As a result its share in total State's own revenue went up from 55.86 per cent in 1981-82 to 83.94 per cent in

TABLE 1

Overall Financial Position of the State

(Rs. in Crore)

	1981-82	1982-83	1983-84	1984-85	1985-86	1986-87	1987-88	1988-89	1989-90	1990-91
A. Revenue Receipts										
(i) State's own	69.12	83.40	93.05	98.16	132.96	136.04	162.73	176.87	207.51	209.80
(ii) Central Transfers	148.24	172.83	199.30	251.85	365.64	364.74	447.06	470.05	453.43	525.37
(iii) CSS Grants	16.85	16.04	24.63	31.72	20.61	33.05	40.02	51.46	60.29	71.46
Total Revenue Receipts	234.21	272.27	316.98	381.73	519.21	533.83	649.81	698.38	721.23	806.63
B. Revenue Expenditure										
(i) Non Plan	149.65	178.17	205.17	241.33	292.88	343.14	437.23	566.04	569.81	652.65
(ii) Plan	42.54	47.51	51.52	63.04	80.10	81.99	118.42	131.40	165.67	195.10
(iii) CSS	20.21	37.52	27.58	39.80	38.42	38.94	53.15	70.78	47.02	53.72
Total Revenue Expenditure	212.40	263.20	284.27	344.17	411.40	464.07	608.80	768.22	782.50	901.47
NET	21.81	9.07	32.71	37.56	107.81	69.76	41.01	-69.84	-61.27	-94.84
C. Capital Receipts										
(i) Gross Borrowing	35.60	76.44	46.66	62.63	82.61	88.98	138.12	153.52	201.67	311.32
(ii) Recoveries of loan	2.02	2.09	3.50	3.50	4.51	4.86	5.24	7.97	16.88	5.25
Total Capital Receipts	37.62	78.53	50.16	66.13	87.12	93.84	143.36	161.49	218.55	316.57
D. Capital Expenditure										
(i) Repayment of loan	3.97	4.55	6.45	10.57	26.08	19.44	19.00	22.67	25.35	27.66
(ii) Non-Plan Capital Exp.	2.73	1.79	3.78	1.99	6.44	5.57	5.38	4.71	12.20	4.74
(iii) Plan Capital Exp.	63.00	70.93	76.54	106.18	115.95	135.70	136.03	161.76	152.19	169.46
(iv) CSS	14.32	1.81	13.46	15.06	25.76	30.00	25.13	29.85	18.03	20.83
Total Capital Expenditure	84.02	79.08	100.23	133.80	174.23	190.71	185.54	218.99	207.77	222.69
NET	-46.40	-0.55	-50.07	-67.67	-87.11	-96.87	-42.18	-57.50	10.78	93.88
Total Rev. & Capital (net)	-24.59	8.52	-17.36	-30.11	20.70	-27.11	-1.17	-127.34	-50.49	-0.96
(a) Public Account Net	-2.93	13.05	10.70	9.73	13.77	-9.55	-9.46	69.62	-8.34	38.62
(b) Opening Balances	-9.39	-36.91	-15.34	-22.00	-42.38	-7.91	-44.57	-55.20	-112.92	-171.75
(c) Way & Mean/overdraft	-36.91	-15.34	-22.00	-42.38	-7.91	-44.57	-55.20	-112.92	-171.75	-134.09
E. Loan raised through PSUs										

Table 1 (*Contd.*)

	1991-92	1992-93	1993-94	1994-95	1995-96	1996-1997	1997-98	1998-99	1999-2000	Linear growth rates
A. Revenue Receipts										
(i) State's own	257.86	286.05	368.80	403.02	457.98	544.99	624.87	693.46	794.02	14.40
(ii) Central Transfers	635.08	730.44	1058.37	865.70	1244.58	1391.30	1346.10	1394.31	1580.60	14.06
(iii) CSS Grants	99.48	36.00	37.96	37.64	51.46	55.73	134.48	163.18	135.96	10.58
Total Revenue Receipts	992.42	1052.49	1465.13	1306.36	1754.02	1992.02	2105.45	2250.95	2510.58	14.00
B. Revenue Expenditure										
(i) Non Plan	691.75	818.84	942.49	1173.55	1343.76	1496.33	1857.30	2325.24	2840.33	16.94
(ii) Plan	220.65	257.51	300.80	364.97	480.35	531.98	724.87	873.58	942.73	19.56
(iii) CSS	70.16	69.22	108.21	75.76	80.24	118.57	116.97	135.14	110.04	19.36
Total Revenue Expenditure	982.56	1145.57	1351.50	1614.28	1904.35	2146.88	2699.14	3333.96	3893.10	16.96
NET	9.86	-93.08	113.63	-307.92	-150.33	-154.86	-593.69	-1083.01	-1382.52	
C. Capital Receipts										
(i) Gross Borrowing	170.08	240.84	257.44	462.06	385.37	542.10	1016.05	976.96	1121.85	19.77
(ii) Recoveries of loan	7.02	19.12	8.10	18.34	25.89	16.02	18.27	29.29	17.36	14.58
Total Capital Receipts	177.10	259.96	265.54	480.40	411.26	558.12	1034.32	1006.25	1139.21	19.58
D. Capital Expenditure										
(i) Repayment of loan	61.88	61.91	62.51	63.41	44.99	52.90	60.60	71.04	80.24	16.76
(ii) Non-Plan Capital Exp.	4.12	5.95	11.23	16.60	17.26	21.85	19.01	11.46	15.59	12.49
(iii) Plan Capital Exp.	171.74	194.66	247.93	280.49	353.47	381.76	640.81	620.56	589.72	13.22
(iv) CSS	23.02	25.47	40.96	46.24	47.71	59.01	52.95	36.37	36.47	10.44
Total Capital Expenditure	260.76	287.99	362.63	406.74	463.43	515.52	773.37	739.53	722.02	13.13
NET	-83.66	-28.03	-97.09	73.66	-52.17	42.60	260.95	266.72	417.19	
Total Rev & Capital (net)	-73.80	-121.11	16.54	-234.26	-202.50	-112.26	-332.74	-816.29	-965.33	
(a) Public Account Net	39.11	21.15	43.74	26.72	33.16	89.50	231.68	522.43	3.00	
(b) Opening Balances	-134.09	-168.78	-268.74	-208.46	-416.00	-585.34	-608.10	-709.16	-1003.02	
(c) Way & Mean/overdraft	-168.78	-268.74	-208.46	-416.00	-585.34	-608.10	-709.16	-1003.02	-1965.35	
E. Loan raised through PSUs				219.08	84.38	304.34	305.39		450.00	

Source : State Finance, The Factual Position, Government of Himachal Pradesh, 1999.

TABLE 2

Percentage Share of Different Heads of Revenue of Expenditure in Himachal Pradesh

Year	State's own revenue on % of total revenue	Central Transfers as % of total revenue	CSS grants as % of total revenue	Total revenue receipts as % of total revenue	Gross borrowing as % of total revenue	Recovery of loans as % of total revenue	Capital receipts as % of total revenue	Total receipts	Non-plan revenue expenditure as % of total expenditure
1981-82	25.43	54.53	6.20	86.16	13.10	0.74	13.84	100.00	50.49
1982-83	23.77	49.27	4.57	77.61	21.79	0.60	22,39	100.00	52.05
1983-84	25.34	54.28	6.71	86.34	12.71	0.95	13.66	100.00	53.36
1984-85	21.92	56.23	7.08	85.23	13.98	0.78	14.77	100.00	50.49
1985-86	21.93	60.30	3.40	85.63	13.62	0.74	14.37	100.00	50.01
1986-87	21.67	58.11	5.27	85.05	14.18	0.77	14.95	100.00	52.41
1987-88	20.52	56.36	5.05	81.93	17.41	0.66	18.07	100.00	55.04
1988-89	20.57	54.67	5.98	81.22	17.85	0.93	18.78	100.00	57.34
1989-90	22.08	48.25	6.42	76.74	21.46	1.80	23.26	100.00	57.34
1990-91	18.68	46.77	6.36	71.82	27.72	0.47	28.16	100.00	58.06
1991-92	22.05	54.30	8.51	84.86	14.54	0.60	15.14	100.00	55.64
1992-93	21.80	55.65	2.75	80.19	18.35	1.46	19.81	100.00	57.12
1993-94	21.31	61.15	2.19	84.66	14.87	0.47	15.34	100.00	54.98
1994-95	22.56	48.45	2.11	73.11	25.86	1.03	26.89	100.00	58.07
1995-96	21.15	57.48	2.38	81.01	17.80	1.20	18.99	100.00	56.75
1996-97	21.37	54.56	2.19	78.11	21.26	0.63	21.89	100.00	56.20
1997-98	19.90	42.87	4.28	67.06	32.36	0.58	32.94	100.00	53.49
1998-99	21.29	42.81	5.01	69.11	29.99	0.90	30.89	100.00	57.08
1999-2000	21.76	43.31	3.73	68.79	30.74	0.48	31.21	100.00	61.54

Table 2 (*Contd.*)

Year	Plan revenue expenditure as % of total expenditure	CSS expenditure on revenue account as % of total expenditure	Revenue expenditure as % of total expenditure	Repayment of loan as % of total expenditure	Non-plan capital expenditure as % of total expenditure	Plan capital expenditure as % of total expenditure	CSS expenditure on capital account as % of total expenditure	% of capital expenditure as % of total expenditure	Total expenditure
1981-82	14.35	6.82	71.66	1.34	0.92	21.25	4.83	28.34	100.00
1982-83	13.88	10.96	76.90	1.33	0.52	20.72	0.53	23.10	100.00
1983-84	13.40	7.17	73.93	1.68	0.98	19.91	3.50	26.07	100.00
1984-85	13.19	8.33	72.01	2.21	0.42	22.21	3.15	27.99	100.00
1985-86	13.68	6.56	70.25	4.45	1.10	19.80	4.40	29.75	100.00
1986-87	12.52	5.95	70.87	2.97	0.85	20.72	4.58	39.13	100.00
1987-88	14.91	6.69	76.64	2.39	0.68	17.12	3.16	23.36	100.00
1988-89	13.31	7.17	77.82	2.30	0.48	16.39	3.02	22.18	100.00
1989-90	16.73	4.75	79.02	2.56	1.23	15.37	1.82	20.98	100.00
1990-91	17.36	4.78	80.19	2.46	0.42	15.07	1.85	19.81	100.00
1991-92	17.75	5.64	79.03	4.98	0.33	13.81	1.85	20.97	100.00
1992-93	17.96	4.83	79.91	4.32	0.42	13.58	1.78	20.09	100.00
1993-94	17.05	6.31	78.84	3.65	0.66	14.46	2.39	21.16	100.00
1994-95	18.06	3.75	78.87	3.14	0.82	13.87	2.29	20.13	100.00
1995-96	20.29	3.39	80.43	1.90	0.73	14.93	2.01	19.57	100.00
1996-97	19.98	4.45	80.64	1.99	0.82	14.34	2.22	19.36	100.00
1997-98	20.87	3.37	77.73	1.75	0.55	18.45	1.52	22.27	100.00
1998-99	21.45	3.32	81.85	1.74	0.28	15.23	0.90	18.15	100.00
1999-2000	20.43	2.38	84.36	1.74	0.34	12.78	0.79	15.64	100.00

Source : Compiled on the basis of data given in table 1.

1999-2000 (table 3). In contrast to it, non-tax revenue rose just by 8.60 per cent per annum during this period.

The tax revenue registered an exceptionally high increase in 1985-86 due to the recovery of huge sales tax, inflating this figure abnormally. In spite of registering high growth rate, tax revenue as a percentage of SDP has been hovering around 7 per cent and this is quite low as compared to 9 per cent which has been laid down for the nation as a whole.

TABLE 3

Tax and Non-Tax Revenue in Himachal Pradesh

(Rs. in Crore)

Years	Tax Revenue	Non-tax Revenue	Total	% share of T.R. in State Own Revenue	% share of NTR in State Own Revenue
1981-82	38.61	30.51	69.12	55.86	44.14
1982-83	44.99	38.41	83.40	53.94	46.06
1983-84	51.11	41.94	93.05	54.93	45.07
1984-85	57.83	40.33	98.16	58.91	41.09
1985-86	73.65	59.31	132.96	55.39	44.61
1986-87	92.40	43.64	136.04	67.92	32.08
1987-88	103.28	59.45	162.73	63.47	36.53
1988-89	118.10	58.77	176.87	66.77	33.23
1989-90	141.96	65.55	207.51	68.41	31.59
1990-91	160.90	48.90	209.80	76.69	23.31
1991-92	192.44	65.42	257.86	74.63	25.37
1992-93	221.67	64.38	286.05	77.49	22.51
1993-94	255.74	113.06	368.80	69.34	30.66
1994-95	299.45	103.57	403.02	74.30	25.70
1995-96	341.52	116.46	457.98	74.57	25.43
1996-97	412.11	132.88	544.99	75.62	24.38
1997-98	476.16	148.71	624.87	76.20	23.80
1998-99	572.03	121.43	693.46	82.49	17.51
1999-00 (L.E.)	66.52	127.50	794.02	83.94	16.06
Linear growth rate	17.11	8.60	14.40		

Source : As given in table 1.

As far as the share of non-tax revenue in the State's own revenue is concerned it is subject to great fluctuations. This is mainly on account of uneven forest royalty receipts of the Forest Corporation. Non-tax revenue has continued to remain at a very low level due to very small user charges in different departments of the government. For example, user charges are very low, and have continued to be low in the past also in the departments like water supply, irrigation, health, education and so on. There has been by and large no change in their rates during the concerned period.

Central transfers to the State went up from Rs. 148.24 crores in 1981-82 to Rs. 1580 crores in 1999-2000, registering a linear growth rate of 14.06 per cent per annum. However this growth does not appear to follow any regular pattern. This can be better explained in terms of devolution of resources taking place through the Finance Commission and revenue component of the Central Plan transfers shown in table 4. The Table reveals that as far the devolution of resources on the recommendations of the Finance Commission is concerned, the maximum increase has registered in the first year of the Finance Commission recommendations. For example in 1984-85 (when 8th Finance Commission became operative), in 1989-90 (when 9th Finance Commission became effective) and in 1995-96 (with the beginning of 10th Finance Commission) a very big jump in Central transfers as compared to the respective preceding years was noticed. However, lately on account of fall in Central excise duties, State's share in Central transfers has also come down, but then this has been partly neutralized on account of increased share of the State in income tax transfers, which have come under Voluntary Disclosure Scheme.

Plan grants which registered 13.79 per cent linear growth rate per annum during the period under study (table 4) too, did not increase consistently over the period under study. For example in the year 1986-87 plan grants were less as compared to the previous year. It so happened that the State had overdrawn from the overall Seventh Plan quota in 1985-86. Similarly in the years 1988-89 and 1989-90 also this figure was less as compared to their respective previous years. In contrast to it, in 1993-94, plan

TABLE 4

Finance Commission Devolution and Plan Grants

(Rs. in Crores)

Years	Finance Commission Devolution	Plan Grants	Total	% of Finance Commission Devolution in Total transfers	% of Plan Grants in Total transfers	Total
1981-82	68.10	71.85	139.95	48.66	51.34	100
1982-83	71.47	77.80	149.27	47.88	52.12	100
1983-84	79.65	93.21	172.86	46.08	53.92	100
1984-85	126.30	102.01	228.31	55.32	44.68	100
1985-86	128.61	158.70	287.31	44.76	55.24	100
1986-87	180.77	153.67	334.44	54.05	45.95	100
1987-88	191.55	211.74	403.29	47.50	52.50	100
1988-89	199.95	199.49	399.44	50.06	49.94	100
1989-90	252.89	171.56	424.45	59.58	40.42	100
1990-91	302.56	212.68	515.24	58.72	41.28	100
1991-92	349.60	268.60	618.20	56.55	43.45	100
1992-93	380.90	339.41	720.31	52.88	47.12	100
1993-94	387.99	650.13	1038.12	37.37	62.63	100
1994-95	465.83	389.74	855.57	54.45	45.55	100
1995-96	724.67	484.60	1209.27	59.93	40.07	100
1996-97	713.64	547.71	1261.35	56.58	43.42	100
1997-98	760.89	485.59	1246.48	61.04	39.96	100
1998-99	727.74	644.15	1371.89	53.05	46.95	100
1999-00 (L.E.)	823.41	733.82	1557.23	52.88	47.12	100
Linear growth rate	15.74	13.79	14.84			

Source : As given in table 1.

grants registered almost hundred per cent increase as compared to its previous year. In fact his was a period of President's rule in Himachal Pradesh and Government of India with an object to cover the resource gap went for an advance plan grant of Rs. 268.74 crores. However, on account of the start of adjustment of the advance given in 1993-94, the grants registered a marked fall in 1994-95. In the following years though plan grants continued to increase (except 1997-98) yet because of adjustment of advance the plan assistance marked very small rate of increase in the period starting from 1995-96. The statistics point out that though there appears to be a decline in the rate of Central transfers, whether they are from the Finance Commission or Planning Commission, yet it is not a secular decline. Though on account of Ninth Finance Commission's recommendations, the percentage share of devolution of resources had come down yet it was compensated by the Tenth Finance Commission.[2]

Revenue expenditure in Himachal Pradesh which stood at Rs. 212.40 crores in 1981-82, rose to Rs. 3893.10 crores in 1999-2000, thereby exhibiting a linear growth rate of 16.96 per cent per annum as depicted in table 1. Thus, revenue expenditure registered higher increase than revenue receipts. Revenue expenditure formed 71.66 per cent of total expenditure in 1981-82, but subsequently rose to 84.36 per cent of total expenditure in 1999-2000. Till the year 1987-88, revenue expenditure was not alarming and a cause of worry, as it was easily met out of revenue receipts. However, from 1988-89 onwards the situation became serious when in order to finance revenue expenditure capital receipts started being used. In 1999-2000 revenue expenditure as percentage of SDP was as high as 42.53 per cent.

The analysis in terms of plan and non-plan revenue expenditure revealed that plan expenditure in spite of exhibiting a higher growth rate (19.56 per cent) than non-plan (16.94 per cent), continued to remain very small as compared to the latter one.

There are many reasons responsible for such a high level of revenue expenditure in the State. Starting from the initial period under study that is from 1981-82 to 1985-86, the high level of expenditure can be mainly attributed to high amount of expenditure on natural calamities. But in the subsequent years, the most important contributing factor of growing revenue expenditure appears to be the ever-increasing burden of the State's wage bill. Fourth Pay Commission became effective from 1.1.1986 leading

2. Government of Himachal Pradesh, State Finances, The Factual Position, Department of Finance, Shimla, 1999, p. 9.

to enhanced pay scales, growing burden of D.A. instalments and high inflation. The situation worsened further, more particularly from the year 1994-95. Certain populist policies like, regularization of daily wagers, pay and pension revision (on account of Fifth Pay Commission Report), opening of some new non-viable institutions, etc. have further aggravated the financial crisis in the State.

One of the most important reasons for such a high level of unsustainable revenue expenditure in the State is that level of Government employment as a proportion of total population is the highest in the country. For example, in adjoining States like Punjab and U.P., this is less than one and two per cent respectively, whereas in Himachal Pradesh it is more than 5 per cent.

Expenditure on salaries registered nearly three-times increase during the period 1993-94 to 1999-2000, exhibiting a linear growth rate of 17.93 per cent per annum during these years (table 5). Expenditure on wages stood at nearly 20 per cent of SDP in the year 2000, and this comes out to be more than double the average of 9 per cent for other major 14 States of the country.

TABLE 5

Main Items of Revenue Expenditure in Himachal Pradesh

(Rs. Crores)

Years	Salaries	Salaries as % of Revenue Receipts	Mainten-ance	Mainten-ance as % of Revenue Receipts	Pension	Pension as % of Revenue Receipts	Interest	Interest as % of Revenue Receipts
1993-94	546.53	37.30	91.83	6.26	84.48	5.76	209.85	14.32
1994-95	598.86	45.84	204.04	15.62	97.69	7.47	223.72	17.12
1995-96	705.02	40.19	208.24	11.87	118.14	6.73	286.60	16.34
1996-97	810.89	40.70	227.92	11.44	142.25	7.14	314.79	15.80
1997-98	987.79	46.91	270.97	12.86	181.95	8.64	455.71	21.64
1998-99	1338.14	59.44	354.17	15.73	233.49	10.37	604.25	26.84
1999-00	1332.31	53.06	457.17	18.20	460.21	18.33	770.63	30.69
Linear growth rate	17.93	—	24.70	—	29.72	—	25.47	—

Source : As per reported in table 1.

The pension expenditure is having all the more serious implications for future. The pension liability of the Government rose by nearly five-times registering 29.72 per cent rate of annual increase (table 5) during the period 1993-94 to 1999-2000. This rate of increase has surpassed the all other growth rates of different heads of revenue expenditure.

In coming years, with improved health system and life expectancy, expenditure under this head will increase much more both absolutely and relatively. Even at present also burden of pension on the State is much more as compared to other States of the country. The burden of pension was 4.1 per cent of SDP in the year 2000, which was nearly three times more than the average 1.4 per cent for other States. The gravity of the dimension of this fiscal haphazardness in the State can be easily gauged from the fact that whereas in 1993-94, nearly 43 per cent of total revenue receipts were being spent on payment of salaries and pensions, in 1999-2000, approximately 71 per cent of total revenue receipts were used for this purpose.

The State Government infact on account of its failure to procure additional assistance from the Central Government and low user charges, has turned to raising of loans recklessly to finance its committed expenditure. As a result the State's interest liability which was Rs. 210 crores in 1993-94 rose to Rs. 770.63 crores in 1999-2000 (table 4). Whereas in 1993-94 out of total revenue receipts, 14.32 per cent was used for interest payment, in 1999-2000 nearly 31 per cent of total revenue receipts were spent for payment of interest. State's interest liability as percentage of GSDP is also much higher (31 per cent) as compared to major 14 States (24 per cent).

At present, after salaries, interest payment is the biggest item of expenditure but in the next five years (by 2005) it is expected that it will rise to Rs. 2700 crores and subsequently it will overtake salaries at present trend rates.

On account of all the aforementioned factors, revenue expenditure as a ratio of GSDP in recent years has been hovering around 38 per cent in Himachal Pradesh against the average 16.5 per cent for 14 major states.

Thus, as for as net position of the State with respect to revenue account is concerned it was surplus till 1987-88, before plunging into deficit in the year 1988-99 onwards. Himachal Pradesh appears to be placed in irretrievable financial crisis. The revenue deficit (Rs. 1382.52 crores) was as high as 13.57 per cent of GSDP as against the national average of 3 per cent in the year 1999-2000. At the present trend rates it is projected to reach Rs. 3771 crores by the year 2004-05, which will be nearly 22 per cent of the GSDP.[3]

II

Capital Receipts and Capital Expenditure

Capital receipts registered a higher rate of increase (19.59 per cent) than revenue receipts (14.00 per cent) as is clear from the data given in table 1. The percentage share of revenue earned through recovery of loans has continued to remain less than one per cent in most of the years under study.

Like other States of the country, in Himachal Pradesh also reliance on borrowings has gone up tremendously. Government's borrowings which were merely Rs. 35.6 crores, forming 13.10 per cent of total receipts of the state, rose to Rs. 1121.85 crores in 1999-2000 at an annual linear growth rat of 19.77 per cent. On account of such a big increase, its share in total receipts also went up to 30.74 per cent in 1999-2000. Gross borrowings rose abruptly in 1982-83 leading to an increase in its share to 21.79 per cent. This was on account of one time receipt of an overdraft clearance loan of Rs. 36.91 crores from the Centre. After showing a little stability, borrowings rose alarmingly in 1987-88, and as a result, the ratio of borrowings and debt outstanding to SDP stood respectively at 8.03 per cent and 36.09 per cent in 1987-88.

As far as the composition of loans is concerned the largest share happened to be that of small savings, accretions to the General Provident Fund and Plan loans (table 4). On account of revenue deficit which appeared for the first time in 1988-89, and thereafter became an almost regular feature, implied that so much

3. Government of Himachal Pradesh, Addressing Fiscal Crisis in Himachal Pradesh, Department of Finance, Dec. 1999, p. 2.

so that even the revenue expenditure is partially met out of borrowings. In the year 1989-90 Government of Himachal Pradesh knocked at the doors of Government of India to pull the State out of clutches of financial crisis. As a result, the Central Government asked the UTI to help the State, and in turn UTI invested a sum of Rs. 70 crores in small savings instruments in Himachal Pradesh. Further in 1990-91, Government of India again came to the rescue of the State by helping it out of financial difficulties, by granting a non-plan loan of Rs. 15,312 crores, which was to be repaid over a period of five years.

The State's revenue deficit became exceedingly high in 1994-95 and in the subsequent years, *i.e.,* 1998-99 and 1999-2000 it surpassed the manageable safe limits. The State had very little options and as a result government's dependency on borrowings raised by it directly, and those mobilised by Himachal Pradesh State Electricity Board and Himachal Pradesh State Forest Corporation, increased further.

The State Government has been depending upon a plethora of uncommon means to mobilise small savings in the recent years. These included temporary deposits in Post Office accounts, loans raised through PSU's, funds drawn as NJPC equities and kept in PLA, balance in the Passenger Insurance Fund normally kept in PLA and daily wage regularization arrears.[4]

As a result of all this, the government's debt outstanding to SDP is also a quite high in Himachal Pradesh as compared to other states of the country. The Government's debt outstanding to SDP which was as high as 46.15 per cent in 1994-95 rose further to 67.89 per cent in 1997-98 and it is expected to go up to 78.54 per cent in the year 2005, at the current spree of borrowings.[5]

However, the State cannot continue to borrow like this to meet its revenue expenditure. There are other States too, which are also in queue to raise loans. It is apprehended that RBI may

4. Government of Himachal Pradesh, State Finances, The Factual Position, Department of Finance 1999, p. 17.
5. Government of Himachal Pradesh, Addressing Fiscal Crisis in Himachal Pradesh, Department of Finance 1999, p. 2.

impose some strict restrictions on reckless borrowings by the states, or even as expected in coming days some Fiscal Responsibility Act may also be enacted, which could restrict the scope of loans by the State. All this is seriously going to effect the adequacy and availability of funds for the state.

As far as plan capital expenditure is concerned it grew at a relatively smaller rate (13.22 per cent) than plan revenue expenditure (19.65 per cent), and as a result its share in total expenditure also reduced during the period under study. Total plan capital expenditure stood at Rs. 63 crores in 1981-82 and rose to Rs. 589.72 crores in 1999-2000. But its share in total expenditure came down from 21.25 per cent to 12.78 per cent in the same period. Till the period 1988-89, plan capital expenditure always exceeded the plan revenue expenditure. But since then the reverse trend has set in.

This gives a very dangerous signal. It is a proof sufficient enough to predict that difficult days are ahead. The borrowings in the State are not being used for asset creation alone, rather they are also used to finance the expenditure with no real return.

Plan capital expenditure which appears to have grown faster after 1994-95, is partly misleading in the sense, because a part of this expenditure was not actually incurred. A part of this expenditure was of the form of equity contribution to Nathpa Jhakri Power Corporation. But in reality the actual release to NJPC was quite less as compared to budgeted expenditure. Plan capital expenditure also rose after the year 1996-97 on account of start of NABARD funded RIDF scheme in 1996-97. The plan specific loans for plan capital expenditure rose in 1998-99, when in addition to RIDF, huge loans were received from HUDCO. Because of this plan capital expenditure did not register a marked fall as compared to 1997-98.

Whatever plan capital expenditure has been incurred in the State, has not led to any direct return. The investment in water, irrigation and housing has not benefited the Government directly on account of very low user charges.

A substantial amount of plan capital expenditure is made in asset creation and loans to State public sector undertakings. Total amount of investment in the equity of PSUs and cooperative societies stood at Rs. 628.94 crores during the year 1998-99. But how poorly the State is managing its fiscal operations can be easily judged from the fact that as against it, the State registered a dividend of just Rs. 0.53 crores. The State's lending operations are also equally disappointing. In 1998-99, total lending of the State Government stood at Rs. 709.94 crores. If this sum had to yield an amount equivalent to the State's average borrowing rate of 12.79 per cent in that year, the interest earned would have amounted to Rs. 92.08 crores in a year. In reality, the State just earned, Rs. 9.40 crores on this count.[6]

The over-all position of financial scenario is very grim in the state. Fiscal deficit which was just 5 per cent of GSDP for all the States, stood at 17.40 per cent in case of Himachal Pradesh in 1999-2000.

III

Implications and Corrective Measures

The implications of this fiscal scenario are going to be very serious in he near future. Non-availability of timely funds will adversely hit scheduled debt payments, which in turn will further make the availability of loans a difficult task. Road construction and maintenance expenditure will perhaps be most severely hit. If the present State of affairs continue unchecked public and private sector investment will be cut drastically. Water supply, and other welfare schemes will have to be discontinued. Electricity supply in public places may have to be disrupted.

Transportation system will be adversely affected with no replacement and maintenance of fleet of buses. New construction will come to stand still. Both, the index of physical and social infrastructure will be adversely hit. In addition to it, employment level and other indicators of development will also be negatively affected. Because of this kind of State of affairs the efficiency level of governance will also come down. Degree of leakages in

6. Government of Himachal Pradesh, Emerging Fiscal Scenario and Possible Path to Fiscal Stability and Development, Finance Department, December 1999, p. 5.

administration and level of corruption will shoot up leading to a vicious circle of poor performance in the State.

In view of this emerging scenario, it is important that a well planned comprehensive programme of reforms be introduced in the state. Fiscal discipline, coupled with effective governance is the crying need of the hour. It is important that certain harsh decisions in revenue raising should be taken. It is high time that a transparent and exhaustive policy of user charges on the one hand, and a practical policy of royalty on the other, be framed after fresh introspection. Similarly control of Government

TABLE 6

Gross Borrowings of the State Government

(Rs. in Crore)

Years	Small Savings Loans	Provident Fund	Market Borrow-ing	Negotiated Loans	Plan Loans	CSS Loans	Other Loans	Total
1981-82	12.52	10.62	1.93	0.53	7.37	2.63	0.00	35.60
1982-83	14.66	10.53	2.48	1.27	7.98	2.61	36.91	76.44
1983-84	16.68	10.54	3.75	1.58	10.10	4.01	0.00	46.66
1984-85	22.67	13.57	3.62	1.05	12.57	9.15	0.00	62.63
1985-86	26.89	15.88	3.02	0.94	16.42	17.09	2.37	82.61
1986-87	30.06	17.31	10.63	0.00	21.18	9.80	0.00	88.98
1987-88	48.60	38.87	12.26	2.66	22.50	13.23	0.00	138.12
1988-89	68.73	38.60	14.99	1.03	22.28	7.89	0.00	153.52
1989-90	111.81	50.96	13.56	0.00	18.98	6.36	0.00	201.67
1990-91	99.98	62.30	22.74	1.11	21.25	5.54	98.40	311.32
1991-92	65.20	53.09	24.24	1.11	19.72	6.72	0.00	170.08
1992-93	76.80	95.26	23.99	4.48	32.30	8.01	0.00	240.84
1993-94	75.61	116.53	23.99	1.84	33.57	5.90	0.00	257.44
1994-95	266.04	118.03	34.44	1.14	33.21	9.20	0.00	462.06
1995-96	134.20	145.65	40.01	7.57	47.72	10.22	0.00	385.37
1996-97	276.09	129.52	44.00	21.67	54.12	15.10	1.60	542.10
1997-98	648.88	196.59	50.88	41.04	64.53	14.13	0.00	1016.05
1998-99	279.29	270.12	140.02	197.53	68.99	21.01	0.00	976.96
1999-00 (L.E.)	61.00	270.12	183.09	331.10	75.89	10.65	190.00	1121.85
Linear growth rate	18.39	21.93	25.20	30.02	12.89	6.51	5.47	19.78

Table 6 (*Contd.*)

Years	% of Small Savings of Total	% of Provident Fund to Total	% of Market Borrowing to Total	% of Negotiated Loans to Total	% of Plan Loans to Total	% CSS Loans to Total	% of other loans to Total	Total
1981-82	35.17	29.83	5.42	1.49	20.70	7.39	0.00	100.00
1982-83	19.18	13.78	3.24	1.66	10.44	3.41	48.29	100.00
1983-84	35.75	22.59	8.04	3.39	21.65	8.59	0.00	100.00
1984-85	36.20	21.67	5.78	1.68	20.07	14.61	0.00	100.00
1985-86	32.55	19.22	3.66	1.14	19.88	20.69	2.87	100.00
1986-87	33.78	19.45	11.95	0.00	23.80	11.01	0.00	100.00
1987-88	35.19	28.14	8.88	1.93	16.29	9.58	0.00	100.00
1988-89	44.77	25.14	9.76	0.67	14.51	5.14	0.00	100.00
1989-90	55.44	25.27	6.72	0.00	9.41	3.15	0.00	100.00
1990-91	32.11	20.01	7.30	0.36	6.83	1.78	31.61	100.00
1991-92	38.33	31.21	14.25	0.65	11.59	3.95	0.00	100.00
1992-93	31.89	39.55	9.96	1.86	13.41	3.33	0.00	100.00
1993-94	29.37	45.26	9.32	0.71	13.04	2.29	0.00	100.00
1994-95	57.58	25.54	7.45	0.25	7.19	1.99	0.00	100.00
1995-96	34.47	37.41	11.30	1.94	12.26	2.62	0.00	100.00
1996-97	50.93	23.89	8.12	4.00	9.98	2.79	0.30	100.00
1997-98	63.86	19.35	5.01	4.04	6.35	1.39	0.00	100.00
1998-99	28.59	27.65	14.33	20.22	7.06	2.15	0.00	100.00
1999-00 (L.E.)	5.44	24.08	16.32	29.51	6.76	0.95	16.94	100.00
Linear growth rate								

Source : As per table 1.

expenditure coupled with efficient use of scarce resources should become stringent policy guidelines. It is essential that a change in attitudes, with respect to viewing Government as a means of employment generative authority and creating all kinds of social infrastructure, should take place. Greater but selective participation of private sector can also to some extent give a sigh of relief to already ailing financial health of the state.

There is a need of reappraisal of departmental schemes and functions. Reforms of public sector undertakings especially with respect to HPSEB and HRTC is the utmost requirement. Role of local governments should be further expanded and strengthened with a view to ensure both more accountability and cost effectiveness. If the Government is having a strong will and determination, the State can be expected to come out of this difficult situation.

SOURCES

1. Sharda N.K. (1986) : *State Finance and Regional Development in India*, Deep and Deep Publication, New Delhi.
2. Government of Himachal Pradesh (1999) : *Addressing Fiscal Crisis in Himachal Pradesh*, Department of Finance, Shimla.
3. Government of Himachal Pradesh (1999) : *Emerging Fiscal Scenario and Possible Path of the Fiscal Stability Development*, Department of Finance, Shimla.
4. Government of Himachal Pradesh (1999) : *State Finances, The Factual Position*, Department of Finance, Shimla.
5. Government of Himachal Pradesh : *Budget at a Glance*, from 1981 to 2000.
6. Government of Himachal Pradesh : *Statistical Outline of Himachal Pradesh*, from 1981 to 2000.

10

BUDGETARY TRENDS AND REVENUE DEFICITS IN DIFFERENT STATES

—R.K. Bansal

The problem of fiscal deficit is not confined to the Union Government alone, the States are facing it more acutely. The fiscal deficit first appeared at the Central level in 1979 but the States followed suit only in 1984. In the current year the fiscal deficit of the States may be 3.9 per cent compared to 5.6 per cent of the GDP for the Centre. A chronic gap between own resources and expenditure potentials of the States seems to be an inherent feature of all the well established federations in the world. Such a situation arises because the States have dynamic and expanding functions but they are deprived of productive and elastic sources. The financial position of the State Government has deteriorated sharply in the last few years. Revenue deficits have widened and the State Governments have been forced to resort to increased borrowings from the Union Government as also from the market and other sources. Increased borrowings has resulted in the increasing interest bill of the State Governments. In the pursuit to control fiscal deficit the onus has fallen on developmental expenditure. In this paper an attempt has been made to study the budgetary trends and amount of revenue deficit of different States over the period from 1990-91 through 1997-98.

Methodology

This study has been based on the data collected from the various issues of the Reserve Bank of India Bulletin published by the Reserve Bank of India and the Economic Surveys published by the Ministry of Finance, Government of India. The study covers a period of 8 years from 1990-91 to 1997-98. To study the shifts in the relative shares, we have compared the four years' average of 1990-91 through 1993-94 and 1994-95 through 1997-98. Compound growth rates were calculated by using the formula

$$Y = ab^t$$

Where 'Y' is the revenue from a source; 't' is the time period, 'a' and 'b' being constants. The growth rate is equal to (b-1).

Results and Discussion

Table 1 depicts the surplus or deficit in different States on revenue account. During the first period, *i.e.,* 1990-91 through 1993-94, all the States taken together had a deficit of Rs. 5971.57 crores and this deficit increased to Rs. 12535.53 during the second period *i.e.,* 1994-95 through 1997-98. During first period, the percentage of total deficit to total expenditure for all the States taken together worked out to be 6.57 which increased to 7.84 during the second period. During first period 15 States had deficit on revenue account and 10 States had surplus on revenue account. During this period the percentage of deficit to total expenditure was maximum (17.12) in Punjab and minimum (1.05) in Rajasthan. On the other hand the percentage of surplus to total expenditure was maximum (44.27) in Arunachal Pradesh and minimum (0.27) in Haryana.

During the second period as many as 17 States had deficit on revenue account. The percentage of deficit was maximum (21.50) in Haryana and minimum (3.12) in Gujarat. The percentage of surplus to total expenditure was maximum (37.29) in Arunachal Pradesh and minimum (1.78) in Goa. The amount of deficit thus increased over the period. When the amount of deficit was converted into percentages to total expenditure, it was found that this percentages had increased for all the States over the period.

Table 2 depicts the percentages of total revenue, total expenditure and surplus/deficit to Net State Domestic Product. The percentage of total revenue to NSDP was 17.89 during the first period *i.e.,* 1990-91 through 1993-94 for all the States taken together. The percentage of total expenditure to NSDP worked out

TABLE 1

Amount of Deficit or Surplus in Different States

(Rs. in Crore)

State	Period I (1990-91 through 1993-94)			Period II (1994-95 through 1997-98)		
	Total Revenue	Total Expenditure	Surplus Deficit	Total Revenue	Total Expenditure	Surplus Deficit
Andhra Pradesh	6736.50	6791.17	(-)54.67 (0.81)	10913.68	12270.43	(-)1356.75(11.06)
Arunachal Pradesh	463.34	321.17	142.17(44.27)	762.42	555.35	207.07(35.29)
Assam	2531.25	2355.18	176.07(7.48)	3728.60	3981.81	(-)253.21(6.36)
Bihar	5442.11	6128.65	(-)686.54(11.20)	8131.63	9079.34	(-)947.71(10.43)
Goa	364.36	354.50	9.86(2.78)	810.48	796.27	14.21(1.78)
Gujarat	5245.73	5616.20	(-)370.47(6.60)	9234.86	9532.19	(-)297.33(3.12)
Haryana	2503.58	2496.86	6.72(0.27)	5665.57	7217.39	(-)1551.82(21.50)
Himachal Pradesh	1079.17	1095.28	(-)16.11(1.47)	1792.59	2015.80	(-)223.21(11.07)
Jammu and Kashmir	1764.88	1580.18	184.70(11.69)	3454.43	2804.16	650.27(23.19)
Karnataka	5103.49	5181.29	(-)77.80(1.50)	9137.84	9445.00	(-)307.16(3.25)
Kerala	3123.97	3497.73	(-)373.76(10.69)	5965.99	6721.17	(-)755.18(11.24)
Madhya Pradesh	5858.70	5960.54	(-)101.84(1.71)	9436.70	10157.64	(-)720.94(7.10)
Maharashtra	10569.15	10864.45	(-)295.30(2.72)	18156.28	18804.27	(-)647.99(3.45)
Manipur	476.25	382.53	93.72(24.50)	749.69	662.36	87.33(13.18)
Meghalaya	421.48	392.99	28.49(7.25)	722.53	636.17	86.36(13.53)

Table 1 (*Contd.*)

State	Period I (1990-91 through 1993-94)			Period II (1994-95 through 1997-98)		
	Total Revenue	Total Expenditure	Surplus Deficit	Total Revenue	Total Expenditure	Surplus Deficit
Mizoram	441.50	354.70	86.80(24.47)	657.81	582.61	75.20(12.90)
Nagaland	514.60	529.34	(-)14.74(2.78)	819.74	859.10	(-)39.36(4.51)
Orissa	2684.80	2839.16	(-)154.36(5.44)	4200.01	4918.42	(-)718.41(14.61)
Punjab	2938.77	3545.68	(-)606.91(17.12)	5782.13	6699.77	(-)917.64(13.70)
Rajasthan	4565.26	4613.69	(-)48.43(1.05)	7556.23	8178.36	(-)622.13(7.61)
Sikkim	194.05	162.97	31.08(19.07)	997.39	956.95	40.44(4.23)
Tamil Nadu	6736.51	7905.34	(-)1168.83(14.79)	11299.58	12126.00	(-)826.42(6.82)
Tripura	576.35	559.45	16.90(3.02)	959.46	881.08	78.38(8.90)
Uttar Pradesh	10448.08	11477.11	(-)1029.03(8.97)	15528.78	19264.01	(-)3735.23(19.39)
West Bengal	4983.82	5755.31	(-)171.49(13.40)	8057.76	9829.59	(-)1771.83(18.03)
All States	84914.33	90885.90	(-)5971.57(6.57)	147242.62	159778.15	(-)12535.53(7.84)

Note : Figures in brackets are percentages to total expenditure.

TABLE 2

Percentage of Total Revenue, Total Expenditure and Surplus/Deficit to Net State Domestic Product in Different States

State	Period I (1990-91 through 1993-94)			Period II (1994-95 through 1997-98)		
	Total Revenue as percentage of NSDP	Total expenditure as percentage of NSDP	Surplus deficit as % age of NSDP	Total Revenue as percentage of NSDP	Total expenditure as percentage of NSDP	Surplus deficit as %age of NSDP
Andhra Pradesh	18.06	18.21	(-)0.15	16.38	18.42	(-)2.04
Arunachal Pradesh	76.01	52.69	23.32	72.02	52.46	19.56
Assam	22.72	21.14	1.58	23.09	24.66	(-)1.57
Bihar	20.54	23.14	(-)2.60	22.22	24.81	(-)2.59
Goa	25.48	24.79	0.69	31.65	31.09	0.56
Gujarat	17.00	18.20	(-)1.20	15.50	16.00	(-)0.50
Haryana	16.53	16.49	0.04	22.10	28.16	(-)6.06
Himachal Pradesh	34.28	34.79	(-)0.51	38.67	43.49	(-)4.82
Jammu and Kashmir	50.99	45.66	5.33	64.60	52.44	12.16
Karnataka	18.54	18.82	(-)0.28	20.02	20.69	(-)0.67
Kerala	19.48	21.81	(-)2.33	21.44	24.16	(-)2.72
Madhya Pradesh	18.69	19.01	(-)0.32	19.14	20.60	(-)1.46
Maharashtra	13.88	14.27	(-)0.39	13.43	13.91	(-)0.48
Manipur	51.46	41.33	10.13	52.43	46.32	6.11
Meghalaya	44.53	41.52	3.01	46.81	41.21	5.60
Mizoram	100.17	80.48	19.59	78.78	69.77	9.00
Nagaland	66.06	67.95	(-)1.89	56.17	58.87	(-)2.70
Orissa	21.03	22.24	(-)1.21	20.91	24.49	(-)3.58
Punjab	13.38	16.14	(-)2.76	16.12	18.67	(-)2.55
Rajasthan	21.04	21.26	(-)0.22	19.93	21.57	(-)1.64
Sikkim	76.47	64.22	12.25	234.13	224.64	9.49
Tamil Nadu	18.61	21.84	(-)3.23	18.53	19.89	(-)1.36
Tripura	54.03	52.44	1.59	63.03	57.88	5.15
Uttar Pradesh	17.61	19.34	(-)1.73	17.22	21.36	(-)4.14
West Bengal	13.22	15.27	(-)2.05	12.85	15.68	(-)2.83
All States	17.89	19.15	(-)1.26	18.61	20.20	(-)1.59

to be 19.15 for the same period. It meant that for all the States taken together 1.26 per cent of the NSDP was deficit on revenue account. The inter-State comparison showed that the percentage of deficit to NSDP was maximum (3.23) in Tamil Nadu and minimum (0.15) in Andhra Pradesh. The percentage of surplus to NSDP was maximum (23.32) in Arunachal Pradesh and minimum (0.04) in Haryana.

During the second period the percentage of total revenue, total expenditure and deficit/surplus to NSDP increased to 18.61, 20.20 and 1.59 respectively. During this period, the percentage of deficit to NSDP was maximum (6.06) in Haryana and minimum (0.48) in Maharashtra. But the percentage of surplus was maximum (19.56) in Arunachal Pradesh and minimum (0.56) in Goa. Further over the period the percentage of deficit to NSDP has increased for almost all the States whereas the amount of surplus has decreased for all the States. Thus, there was a general tendency of growing deficit or declining surplus, if any, for all the States.

Table 3 explains the percentage share of States' own tax and non-tax revenue to total revenue. Considering the four years' average for 1990-91 through 1993-94, this percentage was found to be 59.70 for all the States taken together. This meant that the States had to depend on the Union Government to the tune of 40.30 per cent of their total revenue. During the period 1994-95 through 1997-98, the percentage share of State's own tax and non-tax revenue rose to 62.50. The inter-State comparison showed that during the first period, the percentage contribution of State's own tax and non-tax revenue was the highest in Haryana (82.52) and the lowest in Manipur (8.42). The percentage share was more than all State's average in Haryana (82.52), Gujarat (80.02), Punjab (79.85), Maharashtra (78.60), Karnataka (72.58), Tamil Nadu (69.17), Madhya Pradesh (66.36), Goa (63.59) and Andhra Pradesh (63.50).

Looking at the four years' average, 1994-95 through 1997-98, it was found that the percentage share of States' own tax and non-tax revenue was again maximum in Haryana (86.66) and minimum in Mizoram (7.22). During this period, the percentage share of States' own tax and non-tax revenue was more than 70 per cent in the States of Haryana (86.66), Punjab (84.06),

TABLE 3

Percentage Share and Growth Rates of States' Own Revenue from Tax and Non Tax Sources to Total Revenue

State	Period I (1990-91 through 1993-94)	Period II (1994-95 through 1997-98)	Growth Rate (Per cent)
Andhra Pradesh	63.50	62.07	12.18
Arunachal Pradesh	13.16	12.06	10.82
Assam	33.80	29.60	6.58
Bihar	40.13	40.86	11.06
Goa	63.59	80.94	29.71
Gujarat	80.02	66.45	9.96
Haryana	82.52	86.66	24.16
Himachal Pradesh	26.70	27.94	14.83
Jammu and Kashmir	16.90	13.94	12.73
Karnataka	72.58	73.22	15.93
Kerala	66.36	70.95	19.54
Madhya Pradesh	58.07	59.71	13.44
Maharashtra	78.60	81.37	15.48
Manipur	8.42	11.17	20.20
Meghalaya	15.33	17.04	17.48
Mizoram	13.66	7.22	(-)5.81
Nagaland	8.58	21.92	42.04
Orissa	39.38	43.52	14.67
Punjab	79.85	84.06	19.97
Rajasthan	55.79	60.49	15.74
Sikkim	20.92	69.98	103.62
Tamil Nadu	69.17	74.00	15.74
Tripura	9.03	9.46	14.91
Uttar Pradesh	47.08	49.18	11.62
West Bengal	55.80	58.27	13.99
All States	59.70	62.50	16.07

Maharashtra (81.37), Goa (80.94), Tamil Nadu (74.00), Karnataka (73.22) and Kerala (70.95). In both the periods, States like Goa, Gujarat, Haryana, Karnataka, Kerala, Maharashtra, Punjab and Tamil Nadu had the percentage share of States' own revenue more than the all States' average. In other words these States consistently depended mainly on their own sources of revenue. On the other hand, the States like Arunachal Pradesh, Assam, Bihar, Himachal Pradesh, Jammu and Kashmir, Manipur, Meghalaya, Mizoram, Nagaland, Orissa and Tripura chiefly banked upon the Central assistance in terms of share from the Union taxes and grants-in-aid from the Union Government.

During first period all the States, except Haryana and Goa, which had own share more than the all States' average, had deficits on revenue account. It means that all these States had to borrow to meet their expenditure on revenue account. The two States, *viz.* Haryana and Goa, were able to meet their expenditure from their revenue and they had a small percentage of surplus *i.e.,* 0.27 and 2.78 respectively. However, during the second period Haryana became deficit to the extent of 21.50 per cent and Goa's surplus declined to 1.7 per cent.

The States which had a surplus on revenue account, *viz.*, Arunachal Pradesh, Assam, Jammu and Kashmir, Manipur, Maghalaya, Mizoram, Sikkim and Tripura are those States which had a very less share from their own tax and non-tax sources. During the second period the same picture was visible.

Table 4 shows that during the first period, *i.e.,*, 1990-91 to 1993-94, out of the total revenue, tax revenue contributed 65.49 per cent whereas 34.51 per cent was contributed by non-tax sources for all the States taken together. During the second period, the percentage share of tax revenue increased to 68.41, whereas the percentage of non-tax sources decreased to 31.29 for all the States taken together. Out of the total tax revenue percentage share of States' own tax revenue during period I was 68.50, whereas for non-tax sources States' own share was 43.00 for all the States taken together. But during the second period the States' own share to tax revenue slightly declined to 68.12 per cent, whereas the States' own contribution to non-tax sources increased to 50.16 per cent.

During period I, the percentage contribution of tax sources was maximum for Kerala (78.00 per cent) and minimum for Arunachal Pradesh (23.77). Further, during this period, the percentage contribution of tax revenue to total revenue was higher in the States of Andhra Pradesh (69.03 per cent), Gujarat (71.83

TABLE 4

Percentage Share of Tax Revenue and Non-Tax Revenue in Different States

State	Period I (1990-91 through 1993-94)						Period II (1994-95 through 1997-98)					
	Tax Revenue			Non-Tax Revenue			Tax Revenue			Non-Tax Revenue		
	O	CS	Total	O	CS	Total	O	CS	Total	O	CS	Total
Andhra Pradesh	69.48	30.52	69.03	50.17	49.83	30.97	66.24	33.76	71.16	51.78	48.22	28.84
Arunachal Pradesh	3.46	96.54	23.10	16.07	83.93	76.90	4.29	95.71	23.74	14.49	85.51	76.26
Assam	46.60	53.40	43.94	23.77	76.23	56.06	41.49	58.51	49.56	17.93	82.07	50.44
Bihar	40.93	59.07	64.68	38.66	61.34	35.32	38.18	61.82	73.80	48.43	51.57	26.20
Goa	66.23	33.77	54.85	60.37	39.63	45.15	76.34	23.66	46.37	84.92	15.08	53.63
Gujarat	84.20	15.80	71.83	69.29	30.71	28.17	65.48	34.52	75.22	69.41	30.59	24.78
Haryana	85.06	14.94	63.46	78.10	21.90	36.54	84.00	16.00	45.25	88.84	11.16	54.75
Himachal Pradesh	45.55	54.45	42.27	12.89	87.11	57.73	43.27	56.73	47.79	13.91	86.09	52.21
Jammu and Kashmir	30.35	69.65	35.43	9.52	90.48	64.57	27.23	72.77	31.50	7.83	92.17	68.50
Karnataka	78.17	21.83	76.10	54.81	45.19	23.90	77.79	22.21	77.52	57.49	42.51	22.48
Kerala	74.34	25.66	78.00	38.06	61.94	22.00	76.73	23.27	81.38	45.65	54.35	18.62
Madhya Pradesh	61.33	38.67	61.81	52.81	47.19	38.19	60.93	39.07	65.80	57.38	42.62	34.20
Maharashtra	83.11	16.89	72.09	66.94	33.06	27.91	85.04	14.96	74.78	70.49	29.51	25.22
Manipur	10.37	89.63	33.06	7.46	92.54	66.94	10.41	89.59	33.57	11.56	88.44	66.43

Table 4 (*Contd.*)

State	Period I (1990-91 through 1993-94)						Period II (1994-95 through 1997-98)					
	Tax Revenue			Non-Tax Revenue			Tax Revenue			Non-Tax Revenue		
	O	CS	Total	O	CS	Total	O	CS	Total	O	CS	Total
Meghalaya	27.99	72.01	36.17	8.16	91.84	63.83	25.71	74.29	38.12	11.69	88.31	61.88
Mizoram	3.07	96.93	29.30	18.05	81.95	70.70	3.23	96.77	28.62	8.81	91.19	71.38
Nagaland	10.38	89.62	33.39	7.67	92.33	66.91	45.38	54.62	36.32	8.54	91.46	63.68
Orissa	45.24	54.76	61.01	30.20	69.80	38.99	46.20	53.80	64.51	38.66	61.34	35.49
Punjab	84.16	15.84	68.16	70.62	29.38	31.84	84.78	15.22	56.77	83.11	16.89	43.23
Rajasthan	62.42	37.58	56.58	47.15	52.85	43.42	68.19	31.81	57.89	49.90	50.10	42.11
Sikkim	26.03	73.97	24.05	19.30	80.70	75.95	23.52	76.78	8.76	74.44	25.56	91.24
Tamil Nadu	75.39	24.61	77.88	47.26	52.74	22.12	78.69	21.31	84.26	48.93	51.07	15.74
Tripura	13.90	86.10	39.22	5.89	94.11	60.78	15.46	84.54	37.69	5.83	94.17	62.31
Uttar Pradesh	55.25	44.75	63.57	32.83	67.17	36.43	52.37	47.63	72.78	40.65	59.35	27.22
West Bengal	65.33	34.67	77.59	22.79	77.21	22.41	65.59	34.41	81.24	26.58	73.42	18.76
All States	68.50	31.50	66.49	43.00	57.00	34.51	68.12	31.88	68.71	50.16	49.84	31.29

Tax : O - States' Own Tax Revenue, CS - Share in Central Taxes.

Non-Tax : O - States' Own Non-Tax Revenue, CS - Grants-in-aid and Other Contributions from the Centre.

per cent), Karnataka (76.10 per cent), Kerala (78.00 per cent), Maharashtra (72.09 per cent), Punjab (68.16 per cent), Tamil Nadu (77.88 per cent) and West Bengal (77.59 per cent) as compared to all States' average. The percentage contribution of non-tax sources was more than 50 per cent in the States of Arunachal Pradesh (76.90), Assam (56.06), Himachal Pradesh (57.73), Jammu and Kashmir (64.57), Manipur (66.94), Maghalaya (63.83), Mizoram (70.70), Nagaland (66.91), Sikkim (75.95) and Tripura (60.78). It means that all these States depend more on non-tax sources for resource mobilisation. It may be concluded that small and hill States depend more on non-tax sources to mobilise resources.

During second period, *i.e.,* 1994-95 through 1997-98, the percentage contribution of tax revenue to total revenue improved in the States of Andhra Pradesh, Arunachal Pradesh, Assam, Bihar, Gujarat, Himachal Pradesh, Karnataka, Kerala, Madhya Pradesh, Maharashtra, Maghalaya, Nagaland, Orissa, Rajasthan, Tamil Nadu, U.P. and West Bengal. Further during this period, the percentage contribution of tax revenue was maximum for Tamil Nadu (84.26) and minimum for Sikkim (8.76). During this period, the contribution of tax revenue was more than 70 per cent in the States of Andhra Pradesh, Bihar, Gujarat, Karnataka, Kerala, Maharashtra, Tamil Nadu, U.P. and West Bengal.

Table 4 shows that the percentage share of States' own tax sources to total tax revenue was maximum (85.06) in Haryana and minimum (3.07) in Mizoram. The percentage share of States' own tax sources was more than 70 in the States of Gujarat (84.20), Haryana (85.06), Karnataka (78.17), Kerala (74.34), Maharashtra (83.11), Punjab (84.16) and Tamil Nadu (75.39). It means that relatively developed States rely more on their own tax sources and they get less share from the taxes collected by the Centre. Further, the share of Central taxes to total tax revenue was more than 70 per cent in the States of Arunachal Pradesh, Manipur, Meghalaya, Mizoram, Nagaland, Sikkim and Tripura. But during the second period, the percentage share of States' own tax sources to total tax revenue was maximum 85.04 for Maharashtra and minimum again for Mizoram (3.23). During this period, the contribution of States' own tax sources improved in the States of Arunachal

Pradesh, Goa, Kerala, Maharashtra, Manipur, Mizoram, Nagaland, Orissa, Punjab, Rajasthan, Tamil Nadu, Tripura and West Bengal as compared to the previous period.

The percentage share of States' own non-tax sources to total non-tax revenue was maximum (78.10) for Haryana and minimum (5.89) for Tripura. It may be inferred that relatively under developed States depend more on the Centre for grants-in-aid and mobilise less resources from own non-tax sources. During the second period the contribution of States' own non-tax sources was again maximum (88.84) per cent in Haryana and minimum (5.89) per cent in Tripura.

The growth rate (table 5) for total revenue for all the States taken together was 14.42 per cent. It was more for tax revenue (16.14 per cent) as compared to non-tax revenue (11.98 per cent). The growth rates for revenue transfer from the Centre to the States, both for tax and non-tax revenue, were more as compared to the growth rates for States' own tax and non-tax revenue. The growth rate of revenue from States' own tax sources was higher than that of the share from Central taxes in Arunachal Pradesh, Goa, Maharashtra, Mizoram, Nagaland, Orissa, Punjab, Rajasthan, Tamil Nadu, Tripura and West Bengal. The growth rate of revenue from tax sources was more than non-tax sources in most of the States, but it was not true for the States of Goa, Haryana, Jammu and Kashmir, Punjab, Sikkim and Tripura.

All the States in which the percentage of total tax revenue to total revenue was higher than the all States' average, had a deficit on revenue account. Further, the States in which the percentage of non-tax revenue to total revenue was more than 60 per cent, *viz.*, Arunachal Pradesh, Jammu and Kashmir, Manipur, Maghalaya, Mizoram, Sikkim and Tripura had a surplus on revenue account. However, it was not true only in case of Nagaland. It may be mentioned here that these are special category States where the component of Central grant is substantial. Thus, the tax and non-tax efforts made by the States themselves did not appear to have any impact on the fiscal health of a State. The States collecting higher revenue, both tax and non-tax, from their own people may have to incur extra expenditure to fulfill tax payer's aspirations.

TABLE 5

Annual Compound Growth Rate of States Revenue

(Per cent)

State	States' Own Tax Revenue	Share in Central Taxes	Total Tax Revenue	States' Own Non-Tax Revenue	Grants -in-aid and other contribut-ions from the Centre	Total Non-Tax Revenue	Total Revenue
Andhra Pradesh	12.33	24.29	13.68	29.73	9.92	10.83	12.82
Arunachal Pradesh	20.27	13.80	14.04	10.12	13.55	13.02	13.26
Assam	10.29	16.15	13.53	(-)0.02	9.30	7.29	10.17
Bihar	9.75	15.58	14.27	8.56	(-)1.75	4.61	10.56
Goa	21.33	7.13	17.10	38.85	0.14	27.49	22.12
Gujarat	9.42	41.67	16.52	11.60	11.45	11.55	15.19
Haryana	12.35	14.64	12.70	40.14	14.67	35.70	22.65
Himachal Pradesh	15.57	18.27	17.06	12.84	10.38	10.71	13.53
Jammu and Kashmir	11.79	16.13	14.86	14.31	20.59	19.04	18.28
Karnataka	16.07	16.71	16.21	15.28	12.19	13.91	15.67
Kerala	19.75	15.94	18.81	18.01	9.13	12.75	17.56
Madhya Pradesh	14.25	14.73	14.43	11.88	6.83	9.59	12.66
Maharashtra	16.20	12.10	15.54	13.07	8.50	11.62	14.48
Manipur	12.53	12.43	12.45	24.72	10.54	11.80	12.01
Meghalaya	13.51	16.84	15.93	14.84	12.44	13.53	14.42
Mizoram	11.29	9.79	9.84	(-)7.43	13.74	10.71	10.48
Nagaland	92.39	1.38	14.34	14.10	10.82	11.09	12.34
Orissa	14.00	12.91	13.41	16.19	(-)5.76	9.23	11.84
Punjab	13.35	12.01	13.14	33.15	11.32	27.84	18.44
Rajasthan	16.62	9.42	14.07	14.17	11.07	12.56	13.43
Sikkim	14.04	17.96	16.98	120.90	18.25	57.63	50.56
Tamil Nadu	17.31	11.97	16.07	5.43	3.69	4.52	13.80
Tripura	15.48	11.94	12.46	14.02	14.32	14.28	13.88
Uttar Pradesh	12.69	16.01	14.21	8.29	(-)4.70	2.66	10.41
West Bengal	14.18	13.85	14.07	12.09	6.50	7.86	12.76
All States	15.97	19.36	16.14	16.19	8.28	11.98	14.42

Table 6 shows State-wise development and non-development expenditure. During period I, development expenditure comprised of 67.25 per cent of the total expenditure for all the States taken together. During the second period, the percentage share of development expenditure declined to 62.61 per cent for all the States taken together. During period I, the percentage share of development expenditure was maximum (77.17) in Tamil Nadu and minimum (60.54) in Uttar Pradesh. But during the second period, the percentage share of development expenditure was maximum (61.63) in Arunachal Pradesh and minimum (24.10) in Sikkim. Further, over the study period the percentage share of development expenditure declined in all the States. It means that over the period development works in all the States are getting less priority and States are incurring more expenditure on non-development purposes. Non-development expenditure has increased at a higher rate (19.00) than that of development expenditure (13.08) for all the States taken together. Further non-development expenditure has increased at a higher rate than development expenditure even in each of the States. It was also found that total expenditure of all the States taken together increased at a higher rate (15.18) than total revenue receipt (14.42) of all the States. It was also true almost for all the individual States.

When we examined the development and non-development expenditure and the amount of surplus/deficit during the period I, *i.e.,* 1990-91 through 1993-94, it was found that in the States of Andhra Pradesh, Arunachal Pradesh, Assam, Goa, Gujarat, Karnataka, Madhya Pradesh, Maharashtra, Meghalaya, Mizoram, Sikkim, Tamil Nadu and Tripura, the percentage of development expenditure was more than the all States' average. But when we look at the surplus/deficit, it was found that out of above 13 States only six States, *viz.*, Andhra Pradesh, Gujarat, Karnataka, Madhya Pradesh, Maharashtra and Tamil Nadu had deficit on revenue account. Twelve States, which had the percentage share of non-development expenditure more than the all States' average, nine States had deficit on revenue account.

During the second period, 14 States had the percentage of development expenditure more than the all States' average, out of which 9 States had deficit. Out of the 11 States which had

TABLE 6

Percentage Share and Growth Rates of Development and Non-Development Expenditure in Different States

State	Percentage share				Growth Rate		
	Period I (1990-91 through 1993-94)		Period II (1994-95 through 1997-98)		Development Expenditure	Non-Development Expenditure	Total Expenditure
	Development expenditure	Non-Development expenditure	Development expenditure	Non-Development expenditure			
Andhra Pradesh	70.55	29.45	68.00	32.00	14.89	19.13	15.10
Arunachal Pradesh	72.02	27.98	71.63	28.37	14.61	15.16	14.77
Assam	67.76	32.24	63.84	36.16	12.32	17.32	14.03
Bihar	63.37	36.63	59.22	40.78	8.49	13.34	10.32
Goa	72.42	27.58	56.02	43.98	14.81	37.57	22.42
Gujarat	71.57	28.43	69.02	30.98	13.06	16.56	14.14
Haryana	61.87	38.13	56.45	43.55	27.48	34.85	30.71
Himachal Pradesh	66.36	33.64	66.29	33.71	16.45	16.54	16.47
Jammu and Kashmir	62.30	37.70	60.17	39.83	14.42	17.02	15.42
Karnataka	69.39	30.61	67.75	32.25	15.57	17.80	16.20
Kerala	62.45	37.55	61.14	38.86	17.03	18.67	17.74
Madhya Pradesh	71.26	28.74	67.97	32.03	12.76	17.24	14.26

Table 6 (*Contd.*)

State	Percentage share				Growth Rate		
	Period I (1990-91 through 1993-94)		Period II (1994-95 through 1997-98)		Development Expenditure	Non-Development Expenditure	Total Expenditure
	Development expenditure	Non-Development expenditure	Development expenditure	Non-Development expenditure			
Maharashtra	68.79	31.21	66.54	33.46	13.74	16.71	14.70
Manipur	65.69	34.31	65.12	34.88	14.46	15.18	14.81
Meghalaya	70.75	29.25	67.80	32.20	11.60	15.54	12.89
Mizoram	73.37	26.63	70.20	29.80	11.97	16.43	13.31
Nagaland	62.27	37.73	58.41	41.59	11.07	15.65	12.87
Orissa	66.73	33.27	63.28	36.72	13.31	17.70	14.73
Punjab	63.19	36.81	49.55	50.45	10.37	26.89	17.24
Rajasthan	66.53	33.47	61.65	38.35	13.22	19.39	15.39
Sikkim	74.45	25.55	24.10	75.90	17.41	104.37	55.67
Tamil Nadu	77.17	22.83	67.94	32.06	8.24	21.65	14.23
Tripura	69.27	30.73	67.93	32.07	11.37	13.12	12.02
Uttar Pradesh	60.54	39.46	55.23	44.77	11.66	17.47	13.82
West Bengal	65.45	34.55	61.96	38.04	12.94	17.29	14.32
All States	67.25	32.75	62.61	37.39	13.08	19.00	15.15

the percentage of non-development expenditure more than the all States' average, 8 States had deficit. From the above analysis no consistent conclusion can be drawn, but the States in which the percentage of non-development expenditure was more than all the States' average, they had more instinct towards deficit. In other words, non-development expenditure is main culprit of deficit budgets.

Conclusions

The study reveals that the amount of budget deficit as well as revenue deficit had increased over the period. When the amount of deficit was converted into percentages to total expenditure, it was found that this percentages had increased for all the States over the period. Further, over the period the percentage of deficit to NSDP has increased for almost all the States whereas the amount of surplus, if it existed in any state, has decreased for all the states. Thus an increasing tendency of growing budget deficit or declining surplus has been observed for all the states. The States which have been increasingly taxing their own people are no exception. Perhaps these States have to spend more in order to fulfil the aspirations of the tax payers. Further, the relatively underdeveloped States depend more on the Centre for grants-in-aid and mobilize less resources from own non-tax sources. Also, the States which have been experiencing surpluses, which too are declining, were relying more on the Central grants. This may be the reason for the growing tendency on the part of the States to demand an increasing share from Central resources. In order to check this tendency perhaps some incentive may have to be given to the States to step up their tax and non-tax efforts. States alone do not appear to be at fault for the increasing deficit in the economy. Further, the States' in which the percentage of non-development expenditure was more than the all States' average, they had more instinct toward deficit. This implies that efforts on the better management of State expenditure are also called for. Thus, to contain the deficit in different States a holistic approach is the need of the hour.

APPENDIX I

Net State Domestic Product at Current Prices in Different States

(Rs. Crores)

State	Period I (1990-91 through 1993-94)	Period II (1994-95 through 1997-98)
Andhra Pradesh	37288.50	66625.67
Arunachal Pradesh	609.50	1058.67
Assam	11141.50	16148.33
Bihar	26489.50	36602.00
Goa	1430.00	2561.00
Gujarat	30855.00	59585.67
Haryana	15145.25	25632.67
Himachal Pradesh	3148.00	4635.50
Jammu and Kashmir	3461.00	5347.33
Karnataka	27531.00	45640.00
Kerala	16034.50	27824.00
Madhya Pradesh	31350.75	49297.00
Maharashtra	76119.50	135234.67
Manipur	925.50	1430.00
Meghalaya	946.50	1543.67
Mizoram	440.75	835.00
Nagaland	779.00	1459.33
Orissa	12767.00	20085.00
Panjab	21964.50	35877.33
Rajasthan	21696.25	37920.00
Sikkim	253.75	426.00
Tamil Nadu	36194.50	60963.67
Tripura	1066.75	152.33
Uttar Pradesh	59333.75	90170.00
West Bengal	37698.00	62696.00
All States	474670.25	791121.00

Source : *Indian Economic Survey.*

Appendix IIA

Tax and Non-Tax Revenue in Different States (1990-91 through 1993-94)

(Rs. in lakhs)

State	Tax Revenue			Non-Tax Revenue			Total Revenue
	States' Own Tax Revenue	Share in Central Taxes	Total Tax Revenue	States' Own Non-Tax Revenue	Grants-in-aid and other contributions from the Centre	Total Non-Tax Revenue	
Andhra Pradesh	323097	141904	465001	104681	103968	208649	673650
Arunachal Pradesh	371	10333	10704	5726	29904	35630	46334
Assam	51821	59394	111215	33739	108171	141910	253125
Bihar	144084	207914	351958	76302	117911	192213	544211
Goa	13237	5749	19986	9932	6518	16450	36436
Gujarat	317289	59530	376819	102381	45373	147754	524573
Haryana	135138	23744	158882	71446	20030	91476	250358
Himachal Pradesh	20781	24839	45620	8029	54268	62297	107917
Jammu and Kashmir	18973	43548	62521	10855	103112	113967	176488
Karnataka	303562	84755	388357	66867	55125	121992	510349
Kerala	181153	62521	243674	26154	42569	68723	312397
Madhya Pradesh	222071	140031	362102	118172	105596	223768	585870
Maharashtra	633278	128688	761966	197446	97503	294949	1056915

Appendix II A (*contd.*)

State	Tax Revenue			Non-Tax Revenue			Total Revenue
	States' Own Tax Revenue	Share in Central Taxes	Total Tax Revenue	States' Own Non-Tax Revenue	Grants-in-aid and other contributions from the Centre	Total Non-Tax Revenue	
Manipur	1633	14112	15745	2379	29501	31880	47625
Meghalaya	4267	10977	15244	2195	24709	26904	42148
Mizoram	397	12538	12935	5635	25580	31215	44150
Nagaland	1784	15398	17182	2630	31648	34278	51460
Orissa	74106	89683	163789	31613	73078	104691	268480
Panjab	168579	31733	200302	66087	27488	93575	293877
Rajasthan	161245	97067	258312	93452	104762	198214	456526
Sikkim	1215	3452	4667	2845	11893	14738	19405
Tamil Nadu	395540	129117	524657	70416	78578	148994	673651
Tripura	3143	19464	22607	2064	32964	35028	57635
Uttar Pradesh	366946	297192	664138	124984	255686	380670	1044808
West Bengal	252630	134067	386697	25451	86234	111685	498382
All States	3809831	1751607	5561438	1259900	1670095	2929995	8491433

Source : *Reserve Bank of India Bulletins.*

* The figures in the table are average of 1990-91 through 1993-94 period.

APPENDIX IIB

Tax and Non-Tax Revenue in Different States (1994-95 through 1997-98)

(Rs. in Crores)

State	Tax Revenue			Non-Tax Revenue			Total Revenue
	States' Own Tax Revenue	Share in Central Taxes	Total Tax Revenue	States' Own Non-Tax Revenue	Grants-in-aid and other contributions from the Centre	Total Non-Tax Revenue	
Andhra Pradesh	514384	262180	776564	163000	151804	314804	1091368
Arunachal Pradesh	775	17327	18102	8422	49718	58140	76242
Assam	76665	108116	184781	33718	154361	188079	372860
Bihar	229097	370985	600082	103194	109887	213081	813163
Goa	28689	8890	37579	36912	6557	43469	81048
Gujarat	454835	239809	694644	158835	70007	228842	923486
Haryana	215334	41013	256347	275577	34633	310210	566557
Himachal Pradesh	37074	48602	85676	13018	80565	93583	179259
Jammu and Kashmir	29629	79201	108830	18534	218079	236613	345443
Karnataka	551015	157341	708356	118102	87326	205428	913784
Kerala	372539	112960	485499	50720	60380	111100	596599
Madhya Pradesh	378333	242610	620943	185167	137560	322727	943670
Maharashtra	1154570	203182	1357752	322739	135138	457876	1815628

Appendix IIB (*Contd.*)

State	Tax Revenue			Non-Tax Revenue			Total Revenue
	States' Own Tax Revenue	Share in Central Taxes	Total Tax Revenue	States' Own Non-Tax Revenue	Grants-in-aid and other contributions from the Centre	Total Non-Tax Revenue	
Manipur	2619	22550	25169	5757	44043	49800	74969
Meghalaya	7084	20460	27544	5225	39484	44709	72253
Mizoram	609	18218	18827	4138	42816	46954	65781
Nagaland	13511	16265	29776	4458	47740	52198	81974
Orissa	125182	145777	270959	57620	91422	149042	420001
Punjab	278311	49956	328267	207728	42218	249946	578213
Rajasthan	298258	139162	437420	158786	159417	318203	755623
Sikkim	2055	6683	8738	67745	23256	91001	99739
Tamil Nadu	749198	202931	952129	87012	90818	177829	1129958
Tripura	5590	30572	36162	3488	56296	59784	95946
Uttar Pradesh	591856	538273	1130129	171842	250907	422749	1552878
West Bengal	429375	225268	654643	40170	110963	151133	805776
All States	6891503	3225474	10116977	2310811	2296474	4607285	14724262

Source : *Reserve Bank of India Bulletins.*

* The figures in the table are average for 1994-95 through 1997-98.

APPENDIX III

Distribution of Development and Non-Development Expenditure in Different States*

(Rs. in lakhs)

State	Period I (1990-91 through 1993-94)			Period II (1994-95 through 1997-98)		
	Development Expenditure	Non-Dev. Expenditure	Total Expenditure	Development Expenditure	Non-Dev. Expenditure	Total Expenditure
Andhra Pradesh	479117	200000	679117	834389	292654	1227043
Arunachal Pradesh	23130	8987	32117	39780	15755	55535
Assam	159587	75931	235518	254199	143982	398181
Bihar	388373	224492	612865	537689	370255	907934
Goa	25672	9778	35450	44609	35018	79627
Gujarat	401951	159669	561620	657912	295307	953219
Haryana	154481	95205	249686	407422	314317	721739
Himachal Pradesh	72683	36845	109528	133627	67953	201580
Jammu and Kashmir	98448	59570	158018	168719	111697	280416
Karnataka	359530	158599	518129	639899	304601	944500
Kerala	218433	131340	349773	410932	261185	672117
Madhya Pradesh	424748	171306	596054	690415	325349	1015764
Maharashtra	747366	339079	1086445	1251236	629191	1880427
Manipur	25127	13126	38253	43132	23104	66236

Appendix III (*contd.*)

State	Period I (1990-91 through 1993-94)			Period II (1994-95 through 1997-98)		
	Development Expenditure	Non-Dev. Expenditure	Total Expenditure	Development Expenditure	Non-Dev. Expenditure	Total Expenditure
Meghalaya	27804	11495	39299	43135	20482	63617
Mizoram	26024	9446	35470	40901	17360	58261
Nagaland	32964	19970	52934	50176	35734	85910
Orissa	189457	94459	283916	311224	180618	491842
Punjab	217733	126835	354568	331974	338003	669977
Rajasthan	306949	154420	461369	380896	236940	617836
Sikkim	12133	6164	16297	23060	72635	95695
Tamil Nadu	610055	180479	790534	823840	388760	1212600
Tripura	38753	17192	55945	59852	28256	88108
Uttar Pradesh	694824	452887	1147711	1063952	862449	1926401
West Bengal	376685	198846	575531	609041	373918	982959
All States	6112077	2976513	9088590	10003710	5974105	15977815

Source : *Reserve Bank of India Bulletins.*

* The figures are averages for the respective periods.

11

RESTRUCTURING OF THE PUBLIC FINANCES AND MACRO-ECONOMIC STABILITY*

—*Y.V. Reddy*

New Realities

(1) With increasing integration between the Indian and world economy, in terms of trade and financial flows and especially private external capital flows, we have to recognise the need for some sort of convergence of macro-economic stability parameters. Most critical are, fiscal deficit and within it revenue deficit and especially monetised deficit, inflation and of course interest rates. So we should consider world trends in say, inflation and fiscal deficit, public sector savings and compare our performance in this respect to judge how competitive we stand in terms of stability and efficiency indicators. While we may afford to be out of alignment temporarily, or marginally, or with reference to one or two of the parameters, we will find it difficult to maintain macro stability if we are too far away on most of them, especially, on the inflation and fiscal deficit front. Today, fiscal and monetary options are no longer driven by domestic compulsions alone; they have to broadly conform to certain internationally acceptable norms of what constitutes the sound fundamentals of an open and competitive economy. I do not think we have much option to deviate from these standards in the medium to long-run.

(2) The challenges for fiscal restructuring also stem from several domestic factors. Reforming the financial sector to augment

---

* This article has been reproduced from the *RBI Bulletin*, February 1999. The editor is greatful to the RBI.

efficiency in financial intermediation is inevitable. Further intensification of financial sector reforms means development of a well-organised and efficient debt market, which cannot be realised without strengthening fiscal consolidation and addressing legal, institutional and technological issues. Hence, limiting the fiscal deficit of Centre and States to a sustainable level is critical for further progress in financial sector reform. This will facilitate further liberalisation of regulation relating to banks investment in Government securities and promotion of a more orderly growth of debt market. Fiscal discipline is a precondition for successful financial sector reform. Incidentally, the concept of public sector deficit which includes Government deficit including those of public-enterprises, losses, technically, its significance when many enterprises get into diversified (Government and public) ownership patterns or being privatised, and when they start operating purely on commercial lines. However, there is an implicit Government guarantee in respect of borrowings by any public enterprise, and thus the magnitude of public sector deficit also needs to be reckoned.

(3) There is now an increasing realisation about the importance of monetary policy, and the autonomy in conduct of monetary policy as well as efficiency in monetary transmission mechanism and these require drastic reduction in the currently ruling high level of Government borrowing which again has a significant bearing on fiscal and revenue deficits.

(4) Economic reform in a broader sense would also encompass realigning of relative functions of Centre and States towards achieving economic prosperity and improving the quality of life. In our context, it means greater emphasis on development of social infrastructure and physical infrastructure. Most of the social, and a significant part of physical infrastructure lies in the domain of States compared to Centre. Expenditure responsibility of States is likely to grow in social sectors; particularly education, health, sanitation and nutrition, even after reckoning with some unbundling as also scope for private provision. Economic reform is not sustainable if expenditure of State Governments is not buoyant in desired directions and this has a bearing on vertical distribution of resources.

(5) On the inter-State plane, the new reality is greater role for market based resources for development of a State. So, while States need to be encouraged to compete for resources in the market, there should exist mechanisms in transfer of resources which would differentiate between ability-consistent efforts and the ability-enhancing efforts. By this I mean States which already have a reasonably developed institutional support base and strong fiscal position can garner resources from market and consequently reduce their dependence on Central transfers. In States where institutional setting is underdeveloped, public policies may have to address the issue of improving their ability to access financial markets, while at the same time augmenting their resource base through transfers to help prepare them towards a greater degree of self-sufficiency. This has greater relevance now than before due to market orientation and has a bearing on equity/horizontal distribution.

(6) Against the backdrop of new constitutional provisions relating to giving financial autonomy and responsibilities to local bodies and its inclusion as terms of reference for the first time for Eleventh Finance Commission, the issues of inter-State and intra-State transfers have assumed a new dimension. In this context, there is an increasing reference to Municipal bonds as a means of financing urban infrastructure, especially against the backdrop of recommendations of the Rakesh Mohan Committee. To the extent these proposals involve guarantees by State Governments, they affect State finances and provide expediency to sate level reforms, and to the extent there is a demand for counting them as approved securities for SLR, it has a bearing on interest rate structure and monetary and debt management policies. Our objective is to reduce statutory preemption. The Central and State enterprises should, therefore, be encouraged to access market on the basis of financial strength and viability rather than through sops like tax benefits and SLR routes which distorts the interest rate structure and hampers market efficiency.

(7) On fiscal deficit situation, we have to be concerned about the total liabilities of governments, rather than marketable debt alone, since this has dynamic and spiraling consequences for fiscal policy and its future sustainability, involves a signaling effect for the market, and is important from the view point of the focus of

rating agencies. While market liabilities would include public debt and contingent liabilities due to guarantees, total liabilities would include, for example, provident fund, small savings, etc.

(8) Against the backdrop of Asian crisis, a new reality in the sphere of management of financial risk for the economy is the need to recognise and monitor off-balance sheet liabilities, whether these are due to banks or Governments. In this context, the guarantees given by the State Governments and Central Government, will have to be assessed and monitored. The focus on such guarantees has increased recently in the context of attracting private sector and foreign investment in infrastructure, especially when cost recovery systems are not fully in place. Managing these guarantees can pose difficult problems at a time when exchange rate is fluctuating and the guaranteed amount is pushing up the external liabilities, as for example in the case of power projects. Another non-transparent way of assuming liability by the Government is to issue letters of comfort which do have the same effect as guarantees for the rating purpose and for the sustainability of Government finances, though such letters of comfort may not be reported in the budget documents.

(9) We have to be also aware of new realities in the Government borrowing programme. Let me draw attention to two critical issues in the Government market borrowing programme. One is the increasing cost of Government borrowings, and the other, the shortening of maturities. Both affect the debt management and monetary policy objectives. While the former is related to the size of the borrowing and hence the fiscal deficit, the latter is influenced by the future policy uncertainties, particularly relating to fiscal policy, and consequently the market preference for short-term Government papers to ward off long term interest rate risk. What is therefore important is a dynamically consistent fiscal policy with emphasis on low fiscal deficit. Another source of high cost fund for the Government is borrowing through the tax-favoured instruments such as small savings and relief bonds, apart from public sector undertaking bonds, which not only affect the overall cost to Government but operate as wrong benchmarks for other markets. These schemes may need a thorough review if we have to move away from dependence

on captive borrowing sources towards retailing of Government securities to a larger investor class.

(10) Abolition of *ad hoc* treasury bills and introduction of the scheme of Ways and Means Advances for the Centre is a major development, impinging on both development of Government securities market and fiscal discipline, including quality of cash and debt management. Adherence to budget assumptions on borrowing programme and to the extent possible, subject to monetary policy considerations, adherence to pre-announced extent to monetisation of Government debt by RBI would be essential if credibility in the new system is to be reinforced.

(11) Finally, in the consonance with the Narasimham Committee-II recommendations, we have introduced risk weights for Government securities for the purpose of assessing capital requirement for the banking system and provisioning norms for unhonoured guarantees as essential measures to promote soundness of financial sector. This could imply greater caution on the part of banks in supporting Government borrowings or granting advances against guarantees. Incidentally, the share of banks in total financial intermediation, and that of public sector banks in total banking system are likely to come down in the medium term. Hence, the extent of what may be called captive investors for Government securities, could be proportionately less in both formal and informal terms. This has implications for the interest rate in funding a high level of fiscal deficit of Centre and States.

(12) As part of economic reform, substantial restructuring of public enterprises has been taking place both at Centre and States and this is likely to be intensified in future. Such restructuring has often meant some immediate financial costs, especially when there is large scale rescheduling of debt, and conversion of debt into equity. These measures amount to impact of not several hundreds but several thousands of crore. There is a potential for serious erosion of quality of assets. This aspect requires intensive analysis for designing a suitable approach to restructuring and it is as important as an approach to privatisation in term of its dynamic impact on Government finances.

Macro-Economic Issues

(1) In the light of the new realities described, revenue and expenditure assessments by the commission should reflect the broad macro-economic concerns of reducing the revenue and fiscal deficit of the combined Government sector. This may require working towards a consensus on the desirable path of fiscal deficit of Centre and States.

(2) While fixing the target levels of fiscal deficits for the combined Government sector, some redistribution of revenue deficits and perhaps even creation of revenue surplus would be needed. This poses a critical task of devising a balancing mechanism by the Eleventh Finance Commission. The major element here would be the incentive system, which needs to be built into the devolution mechanism for transfer of resources. Tenth Finance Commission provided a weight of ten per cent for tax effort in its devolution formula. This may need some review. Also, a revisit to the issue of unutilised tax potential in the States, tax capacities, etc. may be worthwhile. Given the importance of cost recovery of expenditure, an analysis could be made to see if we could build some reasonable incentives for promoting fiscal performance of States.

(3) A 'totality' view of fiscal and financial sector interaction is absolutely essential in the context of new realities that have been described. What we have to keep in mind is the signaling effect that the Commission's fiscal recommendations would have on the financial markets. If there is a clear and credible indication of fiscal consolidation by the Eleventh Finance Commission, it will help smoothening the movements in long-term interest rates. Now, with the growing size of gross and net borrowings of Centre and States, persistent combined revenue deficits and cut in capital expenditures, borrowing costs to Government remain high and sticky. The Eleventh Finance Commission's recommendations can help change the market expectations through the adoption of a more credible approach to fiscal restructuring.

(4) While the Finance Commission deals basically with horizontal and vertical equity in resource sharing arrangement, incentives for tax-effort, and perhaps even cost-recovery issues,

one can raise the question of incentive framework in expenditure allocations also. If education and health are critical for reform, and if the assignment of resources is based on the assumption of increased outlays to such sectors, how do we ensure that the assumption is realised? How should we devise transfer mechanisms that ensure allocation and performance in these sectors? In a way, this is stretching the point, but it is worth exploring to confront the reality.

RBI's Initiatives

(1) RBI has been taking initiatives, in multiple capacities, *viz.*, as monetary authority, as debt-manager of Centre and States, and as banker to Centre and States. There is an overlap, and for that matter even conflict, in discharge of these three functions. Hence, it is difficult to pigeonhole RBI's initiatives. For the present purpose, let me allude to some of the efforts we have taken to improve the quality of information, analysis, and operations relating to Government finances.

(2) RBI has been expressing its views in its Annual Reports on the issue of Government borrowings. A specific proposal of putting a ceiling on public debt has also been suggested in a technical paper on the subject published in the *RBI Bulletin* (December, 1997).

(3) Initiatives have been taken to bring about reconciliation between interests of some well managed States and others in imparting market orientation of State borrowings, in the absence of progress on State Funding Corporation earlier advocated by the RBI. Currently, a State has an option to access market borrowings outside the trance of all States, to the extent of 5 to 35 per cent of annual borrowing programme.

(4) A scheme for consolidated Sinking Fund has been designed by the RBI as a mechanism to ensure orderly retirement of market debt, although only a few States have responded favourable.

(5) In recognition of the emerging problems relating to guarantees, we have constituted a Working Group whose Report is due soon. Similarly, we had constituted an informal Committee

to review Ways and Means Advance System of States. The recommendations of this Committee are under study.

(6) RBI is, separately, studying the implications of management of public account for finances of governments.

(7) RBI has been taking active interest in developing Government securities market, in terms of policy (elimination of ad hoc Treasury Bills), instruments (Treasury Bills of varying maturities and innovative instruments in dated securities), institutional development (Primary Dealers and Satellite Dealers), technology (screen based) and legal changes (Public Debt Act, SCR Act, Stamp Duty, etc.).

(8) RBI is constantly improving interactions with Governments, as for example, through recently constituted Cash and Debt Management Group with the Central Government, and two meetings with State Finance Secretaries conducted recently. The interaction is also continuing through ad hoc groups.

(9) RBI publishes data and analysis in its weekly and monthly Bulletins, which are available at website on an adequate and regular basis. The Report on Currency and Finance and the Annual Report provide the Bank's analysis of Government finances and the policy priorities in this sector. There is an annual study of State Finances published in RBI Bulletin, which carries a wealth of information on State Finances.

(10) RBI has been conducting policy intensive research studies on fiscal and other macro-economic issues through its Development Research Group (DRG) wing and through the medium of its research journal, *viz.*; Occasional Papers, which are available for wider public dissemination. Moreover, the bank provides active research support to Government, Planning Commission and other national institutions on public finance issues. Recently, we have initiated a DRG study on the implications of fiscal deficit for macro-economic stability which should be of use to the Eleventh Finance Commission. As requested by the Commission, we will take up analysis of specific subjects in this study and make it available to the Commission in view of the Eleventh Finance Commission's appreciation of research capabilities available in the RBI.

Comments on Specific Issues

There are strong and somewhat divergent views on the relevance of fiscal deficit, importance of public ownership, advantages of decentralisation, transparency in tax-expenditures and on the issue of insensitivity to market related interest rates. I will briefly give my views on each of these issues.

(1) On the issue of fiscal deficit, what level of fiscal deficit is sustainable is contextual — depends entirely on the context, including in particular, the level of domestic savings, especially financial savings of households, the level of Current Account deficit, the acceptable level of inflation and, of course, the rate of economic growth. More than size, what is important is how fiscal deficit is financed and for what purposes it is used. If it is financed by large order of monetisation, it has adverse implications for inflation with a lag. This has been an empirical fact for us. Dr. C. Rangarajan, our former Governor, has made research based observations on the phenomenon in our country. As regards us, to the extent it is used for financing revenue deficit, there would be no return directly attributable to such expenditures. Further, there is an addition to stock of liabilities without corresponding addition to stock of assets, impinging on future cash flows. On the other hand, if the deficit is used to finance capital expenditures, there is addition to both stock of assets and liabilities, but even then such a deficit will have negative impact as long as the direct financial return to Government on addition to stock of assets is less than cost of servicing of additional liabilities. If such expenditures directly compare with private investment and if productivity in public sector is demonstrably lower than that of private sector in the same activity, there would be a further negative impact. To the extent there is funding of public investment out of such a deficit with clear complementarity to private investments, it is possible that deficiency in direct return in made up by increase in indirect returns. One aspect often ignored by economists advocating large fiscal deficits to fund public investment is the expectations on the part of potential creditors, domestic or foreign, that borrowed funds are indeed used for genuinely productive purpose. It is not merely the advocacy or promise of productive use of funds but expectations of creditors

about such productive use that becomes important if 'preemption' is reduced. The sustainable or defensible level of fiscal deficit should be viewed in the current context of mode of financing and use of funds in Centre and States. Sometimes, it is argued that increased fiscal deficit would help stimulate demand and should not be eschewed. But the issue really is whether this is a sustainable course to follow in the medium to long term. Year-to-year variations may be desirable from the view point of counter-cyclical objectives of fiscal policy but only within the objective of medium-term sustainability. The desirability or otherwise cannot, therefore, the settled in abstract terms, but only with reference to context.

(2) On public ownership also, there have been strong views and it cannot be held that public ownership, by itself is inefficient or for that matter relatively more efficient, be it efficiency in technical, allocative or dynamic terms. Contextually, I would suggest, that there are three inter-related approaches. First, if on ideological and strategic grounds, an enterprise has to be a public enterprise, 100 per cent owned or 51 per cent, there can be no debate. On instrumentalist grounds, *i.e,*, as an instrument of non-commercial objective, alternative ownership patterns and optimisation of results could be examined to achieve such non-commercial objectives, provided there is a debate on desirable changes, if any, in market structure also. Third, and in all other cases, a portfolio approach to ownership rather than ideological or instrumentalist needs to be considered. In an investment portfolio approach, it is not material whether a particular public enterprise is currently profit making or loss making or giving high or low returns. For all predominantly commercial activities, where entry of private enterprise is permitted, portfolio approach appears logical. In a portfolio approach, we can project future cash flows, both with plans for restructuring and without to obtain the Net Present Value. If the present value of anticipated proceeds from privatisation appear to exceed the net asset value, with or without restructuring, then privatisation is warranted. The portfolio approach can factor- in degree of public ownership and control since restructuring option includes consideration of degrees of autonomy also. Such a framework can be applied for public

enterprise in both Centre and States. The real issue is a credible threat of privatisation, which in itself will help improve the efficiency of public enterprise in as much as management and workforce would be motivated to improve their performance toward change of ownership. As a result, it is inevitable that a large public enterprise sector will remain, but with greater dynamism. I agree with the view that, a large segment of public enterprise sector will continue to exist for quite some time because of sheer size of public enterprise now. It could also be as a consequence of costly restructuring to avoid privatisation resulting in continued fiscal burden. In my view, effective threat of privatisation is useful, resulting is some actual privatisation combined with increased level of efficiency in the public enterprise sector, thus reducing the fiscal burden.

(3) On the issue of decentralisation, either a conceptual approach or a pragmatic approach is possible. Conceptually, the case for decentralisation in Government can be made when an optimal distribution of powers and functions between various levels is arrived at and a process of decentralisation is warranted to reach the optimum. Further, decentralisation in some aspects or powers could be combined with centralisation in regard to others while meeting optimal criterion.

In the current debate, there is an impressionistic or anecdotal evidence of need for decentralisation. Empirically, it can be established, that where Centre and States are currently performing same functions (Delhi Electricity or Road Transport), States are seen to be less inefficient both in physical and financial parameters. Quantitative analysis of efficiencies, activity-wise, at Centre/district/municipal/panchayat could certainly be attempted. I will not be surprised if the results vary as between States, with a distinct tilt in favour of more decentralisation. However, real decentralisation is not possible unless the staff is squarely brought under the administrative control of relevant level of Government and democratic process is ensured.

(4) Transparency in budget, especially quantifying, to the extent possible, and presenting tax-expenditures is certainly worthwhile. Ideally, the Eleventh Finance Commission should

work on quantifying tax-expenditures in the last five years at Centre and State levels, recast their budgets on a proforma basis and consider these as inputs for assessing revenues and expenditures. There are also related issues of tax exemption of municipal bonds which has been advocated by some. It is no doubt a standard practice in many countries. In India, however, municipal bonds may not sell without State guarantees, which could imply adverse credit worthiness effects for States themselves. Further, while Centre has been allowing tax exemptions to entities like PSUs for raising resources from the market, no such allowance was made for its own securities, till two years ago. Now, some relief on par with mutual funds is available. One clear way of reducing interest burden and encouraging retailing of Government securities would be to review this issue.

(5) Finally, it has been argued that encouraging borrowing by Government at market related interest rates has not brought about any fiscal discipline since Governments in India are not sensitive to interest rates. Hence, it is argued that we need not pursue this cause. I am afraid I have serious problems with such an approach. At an abstract level, one can argue that accepting over-sensitivity in these matters as a fact helps none except those who are insensitive. Again, at an abstract level, it can be argued that price has both a demand side and supply side. If the whole of borrowing programme is monetised technically, then price is immaterial, especially since seigniorage or interest paid by Government comes back, as dividend from the Reserve Bank of Government of India. But what about costs of monetisation of inflation costs to the economy, which are recognisably high and distorting? Hence, if Government does not pay this price, someone else pays it. Even so, ends of transparency of budget operations are not met. We have to separately reckon such other costs of monetisation. Assuming that there is a mix of monetisation and non-monetisation, not charging market related rates on monetised deficit has moral hazard implications. As regards non-monetised part, some cross subsidisation between the Government and the financial sector becomes inevitable if interest rates are not market related. It is true that for this logic to be convincing, markets need

be developed, but developing markets and gradually adopting market related rates serve the longer term interests of efficiency and any effort in the meantime, to artificially depress the cost of borrowings to Government will not be desirable.

12

FEDERAL TRANSFERS AND FISCAL CAPACITY OF STATES

—Manjit Kalra

India today nearly after five decades of Independence has only four States (Punjab, Maharashtra, Haryana and Gujarat) which have per capita income above the national average. Independent rule of Nine Five Year Plans, Two Annual Plans, Two Rolling Plans, Finance Commission awards and transfer of financial resources from a number of Financial Institutions and Central Ministries has not brought much change in the relative position of States in terms of per capita income, which is at times taken as a sole determinant of economic development. the important question that immediately comes to mind is as to what has the allocation of financial resources from the Union to the States achieved in regard to mitigating the plight of fiscal disadvantaged States.

An economic or functional approach to equitable distribution of national funds among the States should be guided mainly by the consideration of each according to its needs. States do not have equal fiscal capacities, therefore, transfer and financial resources has to be, deliberately and consciously, far greater to backward fiscal disadvantaged States. Horizontal fiscal balance implies the existence of some form of revenue sharing arrangements or equalization grants to remove the inequalities in fiscal capacity, provided that the States mobilize their own resources at a comparable standard of their fiscal capacity.

In the present study by ignoring the non-tax receipts such as fees, fines and profits of public undertakings, the fiscal capacity of a State is equated to taxable capacity of a State. Taxable capacity is both absolute and relative. Absolute taxable capacity is the maximum that a State can collect by way of taxes without producing unpleasant effects. The maximum limit to absolute taxable capacity is the limit of squeezability, where the entire net State domestic product is taxed. But no State can tax the citizens to the extent of taking away their entire income. States must leave some minimum level of income as non-taxable, needed for survival by its residents, as social human-beings. This is the essential consumption and should not be taxed.

Some part of Net State Domestic Product is also required for essential investment, both by the government and the private sector. The surplus, that emerges after providing for essential consumption and investment is the non-invested surplus and is the absolute fiscal capacity available to a State for revenue mobilization. By deducting the taxes already collected, the balance if any, is the potential taxable capacity which can be mobilized through additional taxation.

But it is quite possible that some States end up with negative absolute taxable capacity. The current Net State Domestic Product may be less than required for essential consumption and investment. The transfer of resources from the Union must ensure that the citizens of negative absolute capacity States are provided for, at least, minimum average level of services, at relative tax burdens.

This necessitates the estimation of relative fiscal capacity of States. The relative fiscal capacity of the States is the percentage of absolute fiscal capacity to the Net State Domestic Product. Higher the percentage, higher is the relative capacity of the States. The transfer of financial resources from the Union, must be in accordance with the relative fiscal capacity of the States. The States having negative absolute taxable capacity are bound to be at lower ranks, when ranked on a relative scale. Thus, necessitating proportionately larger transfer of funds from the Union, if fiscal equity is to be achieved, and reduction in inter-State disparities the objective.

The above concept of absolute and relative taxable capacity is based on the assumptions of :

- Closed economy : Inter-State flows of trade and foreign trade of States is excluded.
- Zero substitution effect : Additional taxation will have no adverse effect on private investment.
- Actual consumption is equal to essential consumption for the entire population of the State (AC = EC).

The estimates of fiscal capacity will yield the level of warranted own revenue to be raised by each State to help finance the level of warranted expenditure in the State, by its own efforts. The amount of equalization grant for each State may then be calculated simply as the difference between the warranted expenditure (need) and warranted revenue capacity.

The formula applied for computing the absolute and relative taxable/fiscal capacity is as follows :

$$AFC = NSDP - (EC + G + P_1)$$

$$RFC = AFC/NSDP_{FC}$$

Where

AFC	=	Absolute Fiscal Capacity
RFC	=	Relative Fiscal Capacity
$NSDP_{FC}$	=	Net State Domestic Product at Factor Cost
EC	=	Essential Consumption
G	=	State Government Expenditure both on Revenue and Capital Account
P_1	=	Private Investment

The consumption and usage of these variables in the context of the present study need to be explained. Absolute and relative fiscal capacity have already been discussed.

The Net State Domestic Product at factor cost (NSDPFC) is the limit of squeezability to which the citizens of a State can be expected to pay, by way of taxes, regardless of their suffering. But no State government will do so, as it will reduce to potential taxable capacity of the State by impairing the productivity and efficiency of the factors of production. Essential consumption has to be exempted from taxation.

Essential consumption (EC) is the income necessary for physical survival and maintenance of the efficiency to live as human-beings in a society and work as productive factor of production. Some income is required for social needs, the non-satisfaction of which may impair the physical efficiency. Socially accepted minimum needs are both food and non-food. Poverty line in monetary terms is the best proxy variable for estimating the minimum required accepted 'consumption basket' of the citizens of a State.

State-specific poverty lines if adjusted for current prices would give the required purchasing power to meet the specific calorie intake standard with some allowances for the non-food consumption needs. This is the essential consumption of the residents of a State, which must be exempted from taxation to avoid undesirable effects on production.

State-specific poverty line adopted to purchase the consumption basket differs significantly across the States. The food habits will depend on local availability as well as on consumer preferences. There are bound to be inter-State differences in terms of population structure, climatic and topographical considerations and so on. These need to be reflected in calorie requirements. But to ensure comparability across States the same 'consumption basket' has to be assumed in the base year. The base year for consumption basket is 1973-74 estimated at 1960-61 State-specific price base. Population has been categorized on the basis of residence into rural and urban population.

For population living in rural areas referred to as rural population, Consumer Price Index for Agricultural Labourers (CPIAL) has been applied.

For population living in urban areas referred to as urban population, Consumer Price Index for Industrial Workers (CPIIW) has been applied. Essential consumption has been computed (tables 1-4) for fourteen major States for the years 1970-1971, 1980-1981, 1990-1991 and 1996-97 reflecting the minimum purchasing power required in monetary terms to buy the basic needs consumption basket by the residents of the respective States, representing the four decades.

TABLE 1

Per Capita and Total Essential Consumption of Rural and Urban population

(1970-71)

States	Price Index 1970-71 Rural (1960-61=100)	PCAEC Rural (Rs.)	Rural population (lakhs)	TAEC Rural (Rs. crores)	Price Index 1970-71 Urban 1960-61=100	PCAEC Urban (Rs.)	Urban pop -ulation (lakhs)	TAEC Urban (Rs. croes)	TAEC Rural & Urban 1970-71 (Rs. crores)
1	2	3	4	5	6	7	8	9	10
Gujarat	173	392	192	755	184	539	75	404	1159
Haryana	194	412	83	342	199	488	18	88	430
Maharashtra	192	411	347	1426	191	560	157	879	2305
Punjab	194	412	103	424	197	484	32	154	578
Tamil Nadu	174	382	287	1096	182	494	125	617	1713
West Bengal	206	485	333	1615	183	494	110	543	2158
Andhra Pradesh	171	350	351	1228	194	513	84	431	1659
Karnataka	188	376	222	835	194	506	71	359	1194
Kerala	214	463	179	829	199	543	35	190	1019
Bihar	206	426	507	2160	196	519	56	291	2451
Madhya Pradesh	198	377	349	1316	196	542	68	369	1685
Orissa	212	421	201	846	188	552	18	99	945
Rajasthan	173	362	212	767	187	507	45	225	992
Uttar Pradesh	183	350	759	2656	197	496	124	615	3271

Source : Col (2) : Centre for Monitoring Indian Economy, *Basic Statistics : States. Monthly review of the Indian Economy*, Economic Intelligence Services, Bombay, Sep. 1994, table 13.2

Col (4) & Col (8) : Census of India, 1971.

Col (6) : Labour Bureau's series of Consumer Price Index Number for industrial workers, Ministry of labour, page 145.

Col (3) & (9) : Computed from Appendix I see note I for explanation.

Col (10) : Summation of Col (5) and (9).

Note : PCAEC and TAEC stand for per capita actual essential consumption and total actual essential consumption respectively.

TABLE 2

Per Capita and Total Essential Consumption of Rural and Urban Population (1980-81)

States	Price Index 1980-81 Rural	PCAEC Rural (Rs.)	Rural population (lakhs)	TAEC Rural (Rs. crores)	Price Index 1980-81 Urban	PCAEC Urban (Rs.)	Urban pop -ulation (lakhs)	TAEC Urban (Rs. crores)	TAEC Rural & Urban (Rs. crores)
1	2	3	4	5	6	7	8	9	10
Gujarat	356	809	235	1901	434	1271	106	1347	3248
Haryana	437	928	101	937	470	1153	28	323	1260
Maharashtra	405	867	408	3537	461	1352	220	2974	6511
Punjab	437	928	127	1179	456	1116	47	524	1703
Tamil Nadu	391	858	325	2788	453	1230	159	1956	4744
West Bengal	400	942	401	3777	395	1066	145	1546	5323
Andhra Pradesh	353	722	410	2960	459	1214	125	1517	4477
Karnataka	398	796	264	2101	468	1221	107	1306	3407
Kerala	379	820	207	1697	458	1236	48	593	2290
Bihar	428	885	612	5416	433	1147	87	998	6414
Madhya Pradesh	433	824	416	3428	646	1283	106	1360	4788
Orissa	441	816	233	1901	428	1257	31	390	2291
Rajasthan	425	889	271	2409	473	1282	72	923	3332
Uttar Pradesh	457	874	910	7952	454	1143	199	2275	10228

Source :

Col (2) & (6) : Same as of table Col (2) & (6).

Col (4) and (8) : Census of India 1981.

Col (10) : Computed by adding col (5) & (9) .

TABLE 3

Per Capita and Total Essential Consumption of Rural and Urban Population (1990-91)

States	Price Index 1990-91 Rural	PCAEC Rural (Rs.)	Rural popula-tion (lakhs)	TAEC Rural (Rs. crores)	Price Index 1990-91 Urban	PCAEC Urban (Rs.)	Urban pop -ulation (lakhs)	TAEC Urban (Rs. crores)	TAEC Rural & Urban (Rs. crores)
1	2	3	4	5	6	7	8	9	10
Gujarat	742	1686	271	2569	923	2705	142	3841	8410
Haryana	930	1975	124	2449	973	2387	40	955	3404
Maharashtra	801	1715	484	8300	972	2851	305	8695	16995
Punjab	930	1975	143	2824	960	2349	60	1409	4233
Tamil Nadu	784	1720	368	3600	943	2560	190	4864	11194
West Bengal	842	1983	494	9796	822	2218	187	4148	13944
Andhra Pradesh	657	1336	486	6493	888	2349	179	4205	10698
Karnataka	807	1614	311	5019	996	2598	139	3611	8630
Kerala	939	2032	214	4348	862	2352	77	1811	6159
Bihar	906	1873	750	14047	872	2310	113	2610	16657
Madhya Pradesh	862	1640	508	8331	996	2754	153	4214	12545
Orissa	830	1649	274	4518	758	2226	42	935	5553
Rajasthan	885	1851	339	6275	951	2577	101	2603	8878
Uttar Pradesh	960	1836	1115	20471	960	2418	276	6674	27145

Source :

Col (2) & (6) : Same as of Table Col (2) & (6).

Col (4) and (8) : Census of India 1991.

Col (10) : Computed by adding col (5) & (9).

TABLE 4

Per Capita and Total Essential Consumption of Rural and Urban Population (1996-97)

States	Price Index 1996-97 Rural	PCAEC Rural (Rs.)	Rural population (lakhs)	TAEC Rural (Rs. crores)	Price Index 1996-97 Urban	PCAEC Urban (Rs.)	Urban pop -ulation (lakhs)	TAEC Urban (Rs. crores)	TAEC Rural & Urban (Rs. crores)
1	2	3	4	5	6	7	8	9	10
Gujarat	1356	3081	291	8966	1670	4894	164	8026	16992
Haryana	1325	2814	137	3855	1742	4273	48	2051	5906
Maharashtra	1498	3207	514	16484	1795	5264	351	18477	34961
Punjab	1052	2234	155	3463	1547	3785	69	2616	6079
Tamil Nadu	1480	3247	383	12436	1764	4789	211	10105	22541
West Bengal	1415	3332	537	17893	1394	3761	209	7860	25753
Andhra Pradesh	1297	2637	514	13554	1654	4375	207	9056	22610
Karnataka	1551	3102	333	10330	1873	4885	160	7816	18146
Kerala	1843	3988	221	8813	1732	4726	89	4206	13019
Bihar	1555	3215	799	25688	1500	3974	131	5206	30894
Madhya Pradesh	1576	2998	556	16669	1725	4770	1858	8824	25493
Orissa	1537	3054	292	8918	1354	3976	52	2067	10985
Rajasthan	1605	3357	377	12656	1661	4501	120	5401	18057
Uttar Pradesh	1742	3331	1234	41104	1621	4083	333	13596	54700

Source :

Col (2) : *Reserve Bank of India Bulletin*, December, 1998.

Col (4) and (8) : Government of India, Ministry of Home Affairs, Population Projections for India and States, New Delhi, 1996.

Col (6) : Computed from Statistical Abstract of India, Central Statistical Organization, Department of Statistics and Programme Implementation, Government of India, New Delhi, 1998, pp. 339-345.

State Government expenditure (budgetary expenditure on revenue and capital account) is another variable which has to be deducted from Net State Domestic Product to arrive at the taxable/ fiscal capacity of the States. It is the expenditure incurred by the

State Government both on revenue and capital account. All expenditure on the wages and salaries to the administrative staff of different departments, expenditure incurred on the maintenance of the offices, etc., must be deducted from the Net State Domestic Product to arrive at the taxable capacity of the State.

The major heads of capital expenditure are :

(a) Development outlay on social and economic services.

(b) Non-developmental outlay on the discharge of internal debt, repayment of loans to the Centre and loans to the local bodies and other agencies for social, economic and non-developmental purposes.

In a dynamic world, every economy has to divert a part of society's currently available resources to investment. Investment is required to increase the stock of capital goods, so as to make possible an expansion of consumable output in future. This will enhance the potential non-invested surplus of the State and hence enlarge the potential taxable/fiscal capacity of the State.

India, has both public and private sectors, therefore, both public and private investment has to be deducted from the Net State Domestic Product in order to arrive at the fiscal capacity of the State. Public investment *i.e.,* State Government's budgetary expenditure has already been accounted for (expenditure on capital account).

Now, we have to compute minimum required private investment (P_1) of a State. Two types of investment are required :

(a) Demographic investment is needed to maintain the growing population of the State at the same per capita income. It is determined by the rate of growth of population.

(b) Economic investment is required for raising the per capita income level. This is determined by the rate of growth of population and the desired rate of increase in National Product and Per Capita income. The rate of national income is a function of capital-output ratio. Incremental Capital-Output Ratio (ICOR) expresses the relationship between the amount of increase in output (income) resulting from a given increase in the stock of capital.

Thus, minimum required investment in an economy is :

ICOR x rate of growth of population x desired rate of increase in income (national and per capita).

The value of the above variables for the Indian economy have been estimated and applied to the States.

ICOR = 3.7

Rate of growth of population = 2.2 per cent. Desired rate of increase in national income = 4 per cent per annum. Substituting, the values in the above formula, the required rate of investment is 32.56 per cent per annum.

On the basis of experience, it can be implied that 45 per cent per annum investment is to be made by the private sector. Therefore, the required minimum private sector investment is 14.65 (15 per cent) of national income. Therefore, 15 per cent of Net State Domestic Product has been excluded from Net State Domestic Product to arrive at the fiscal/taxable capacity of the States. This portion of the Net State Domestic Product is not available for taxation. With economic development both ICOR and growth rate of population are bound to decline and then the same 15 per cent level of investment can bring about a higher rate of growth of income.

The rate of increase in per capita income can be obtained by subtracting the rate of growth of population from the rate of growth of national income. In this case the increase in per capita income will be 1.8 per cent per annum for the economy as a whole. The increase in per capita income will ensure higher living standards and improvement in the economic well-being of the people so that they can afford more and better amenities of life. For most people in the backward States, and population below the poverty line, it means having access to more and better food, clothing, shelter, education and medical facilities.

Tables 5-8 reflect the absolute and relative taxable capacity of the States for the years 1970-71, 1980-81, 1990-91 and

1996-97 respectively. Gross and Net Economic Surplus have also been computed. The analysis of the Tables groups the States as such :

	1970-71	1980-81	1990-91	1996-97
States having positive absolute taxable capacity	Gujarat, Haryana Maharashtra, Punjab, Tamil Nadu, West Bengal, Andhra Pradesh, Karnataka, Rajasthan	Gujarat, Haryana, Maharashtra, Punjab, West Bengal, Andhra Pradesh, Karnataka, Kerla	All States except Bihar	All States
States having negative absolute taxable capacity	Kerala, Bihar, Madhya Pradesh, Orissa and Uttar Pradesh	Tamil Nadu, Bihar, Madhya Pradesh, Orissa, Rajasthan and Uttar Pradesh	Bihar	None

In 1970-71 six States out of fourteen had negative absolute taxable capacity. But in the next decade we had two more States Tamil Nadu and Rajasthan also in this group. Thus, 1990-91 started with majority of the States (eight out of fourteen) having negative absolute taxable capacity. The implication, is clear, majority of the States had negative fiscal/taxable capacity on an absolute scale. But the decade 1990-91 ended with only Bihar, having negative fiscal capacity. Again, the conclusion was clear that Bihar had negative non-invested surplus (Net State Domestic Product $< EC+G+P_1$). The position has improved somewhat by 1996-97 with even Bihar emerging with positive absolute taxable capacity and that also higher than that of Orissa. Bihar has Rs. 1882 crores, absolute taxable capacity, whereas Orissa has only Rs. 251 crores, which is much lower than that of 1990-91 (Rs. 945 crores).

TABLE 5

Absolute and Relative Taxable Capacity of the States and gross and net Economic Surplus (1970-71)

(Rs. in Crore)

States	Net State Domestic Product at factor cost	Essential consum -ption	Gross econ-omic surplus	Budgetary expenditure on revenue and capital account	Net econo-mic surplus	Private invest-ment 15% of Col. (2)	Absolute taxable capacity	Relative taxable capacity (Per cent)
1	2	3	4	5	6	7	8	9
Gujarat	2189	1159	1030	312	718	328	390	18
Haryana	869	430	439	140	299	130	169	19
Maharashtra	3876	2305	1571	626	945	581	364	09
Punjab	1436	578	858	189	669	215	545	32
Tamil Nadu	2371	1713	658	401	257	256	99	04
West Bengal	3168	2158	1010	409	601	475	126	04
Andhra Pradesh	2523	1659	864	428	436	378	58	02
Karnataka	1858	1194	664	335	329	279	50	03
Kerala	1255	1019	236	230	06	188	(-)182	(-)14
Bihar	2245	2451	206	336	(-)130	337	(-)467	(-)21
Madhya Pradesh	1991	1685	306	298	08	299	(-)291	(-)15
Orissa	1037	945	92	190	(-)98	155	(-)253	(-)24
Rajasthan	1654	992	662	351	311	248	63	04
Uttar Pradesh	4257	3271	986	516	470	638	(-)168	(-)04

Source :

Col (2) : GOI, Ministry of Finance, *Indian Economics Statistics, Public Finance*, 1991, p. 78.

Col (3) : From table 1, Col. (10).

Col (5) : *Reserve Bank of India Bulletin*, Sept. 1972.

Note : Computed on the basis of formula.

AFC/ATC = $NSDP_{FC}$ – (EC+G+P)

RFC/RTC = AFC/NSDP

GES = NSDP – EC

NES = GES – G

TABLE 6

Absolute and Relative Taxable Capacity of the States and Gross and Net Economic Surplus (1980-81)

(Rs. in Crore)

States	Net State Domestic Product at factor cost	Essential consum -ption	Gross econ- omic surplus	Budgetary expenditure on revenue and capital account	Net econo- mic surplus	Private invest- ment 15% of Col. (2)	Absolute taxable capacity	Relative taxable capacity (Per cent)
1	2	3	4	5	6	7	8	9
Gujarat	6585	3248	3337	1442	1895	988	907	14
Haryana	3032	1260	1772	607	1165	455	710	23
Maharashtra	15113	6511	8602	2613	4989	2267	2722	18
Punjab	4449	1703	2746	816	1930	667	1263	28
Tamil Nadu	7218	4744	2474	1686	788	1883	(-)1095	(-)15
West Bengal	8720	4223	3397	1552	1845	1308	537	06
Andhra Pradesh	7324	4477	2847	1610	1237	1099	138	02
Karnataka	5616	3407	2209	1302	907	842	65	01
Kerala	3823	2290	1533	856	677	573	104	03
Bihar	6360	6414	(-)54	1790	(-)1844	954	(-)21798	(-)44
Madhya Pradesh	6887	4788	2099	1589	510	1033	(-)523	(-)08
Orissa	3225	2291	934	877	(-)186	484	(-)670	(-)21
Rajasthan	4126	3332	764	1120	(-)1875	619	(-)2494	(-)60
Uttar Pradesh	14012	10228	3784	2669	1115	2102	(-)987	(-)07

Source :

Col (2) : Centre for Monitoring Indian Economy, *Basic Statistics : States, Monthly Review of the Indian Economy*, Economic Intelligence Services, Bombay, September, 1994, table 10.4.

Col (3) : From table 2, Col (10).

Col (5) : Centre for Monitoring Indian Economy, *Basic Statistics : States, Monthly Review of the Indian Economy*, Economic Intelligence Services, Bombay, September, 1994, table 12.4.

TABLE 7

Absolute and Relative Taxable Capacity of the States and Gross and Net Economic Surplus (1990-91)

(Rs. in Crore)

States	Net State Domestic Product at factor cost	Essential consum -ption	Gross econ- omic surplus	Budgetary expenditure on revenue and capital account	Net econo- mic surplus	Private invest- ment 15% of Col. (2)	Absolute taxable capacity	Relative taxable capacity (Per cent)
1	2	3	4	5	6	7	8	9
Gujarat	23810	8410	15400	5475	9925	3571	6354	27
Haryana	12263	3404	8859	2395	6464	1839	4625	38
Maharashtra	56856	16995	39861	10821	29040	8528	20512	36
Punjab	16830	4233	12597	3367	9230	2524	6706	40
Tamil Nadu	25916	11194	14722	6607	8115	2887	4228	16
West Bengal	31386	13944	17442	6020	11422	4708	6714	21
Andhra Pradesh	30168	10698	19740	6570	12900	4525	8375	28
Karnataka	20847	8630	12217	4981	4236	2127	4109	20
Kerala	12062	6159	5903	3385	2518	1809	709	06
Bihar	22736	16657	6079	6216	(-)137	3410	(-)354	(-)02
Madhya Pradesh	26349	12545	13804	5937	7867	3952	3915	15
Orissa	11228	5553	5675	3046	2629	1684	945	08
Rajasthan	17804	8878	8926	4130	4796	2671	2125	12
Uttar Pradesh	48962	27145	21817	12306	9511	7344	2167	04

Source :

Col (2) : Centre for Monitoring Indian Economy, *Basic Statistics : States, Monthly Review of the Indian Economy,* Economic Intelligence Services, Bombay, September 1994, table 7.8.

Col (3) : From table 3, Col (10).

Col (5) : Centre for Monitoring Indian Economy, *Basic Statistics : States, Monthly Review of the Indian Economy*, Economic Intelligence Services, Bombay, September 1994, table 12.8.

TABLE 8

Absolute and Relative Taxable Capacity of the States and Gross and Net Economic Surplus (1996-97)

(Rs. in Crore)

States	Net State Domestic Product at factor cost	Essential consum -ption	Gross econ- omic surplus	Budgetary expenditure on revenue and capital account	Net econo- mic surplus	Private invest- ment 15% of Col. (2)	Absolute taxable capacity	Relative taxable capacity (Per cent)
1	2	3	4	5	6	7	8	9
Gujarat	66883	16992	49891	12574	37317	10035	27282	41
Haryana	30363	5906	24457	7893	16564	4560	12004	39
Maharashtra	155388	34961	120427	25005	95422	23310	72112	46
Punjab	40586	6079	34507	7547	26960	6105	20855	51
Tamil Nadu	69042	22541	46501	15402	31099	10350	20749	30
West Bengal	71568	25753	45815	13032	32783	10740	22043	31
Andhra Pradesh	75410	22610	52800	16265	36535	11310	25225	33
Karnataka	51360	18146	32214	11777	21437	7710	13727	27
Kerala	32387	13019	19368	8287	11081	4860	6221	19
Bihar	41188	30894	10294	2232	8062	6180	1882	4
Madhya Pradesh	55872	25493	30379	14216	16163	8385	7798	14
Orissa	20636	10985	9651	6310	3341	3090	251	1
Rajasthan	44307	18057	26250	10964	15286	6645	8641	19
Uttar Pradesh	102864	54700	48164	23017	25147	15435	9712	9

Source :

Col (2) : Economic Advisor, Punjab, *Statistical Abstract*, 1999.

Col (3) : From table 4, Col (10).

Col (5) : GOI, *Reserve Bank of India Bulletin*, Feb. 1999.

To analyse the role of Finance Commissions in the reduction in inter-State disparities, ranking of the per capita State-wise transfers has been computed in table 9. Financial transfers are aggregated till 1988-89 (Appendix 5). The coefficient of rank correlation is estimated with respect to per capita income 1970-71, 1980-81, 1990-91 and 1996-97. Since the impact of federal transfers would be visible only after a time lag, therefore, coefficient of rank correlation has also been computed for 1990-91 and 1996-97.

The important trends that emerge from the analysis of table 9 are :

- The coefficient of rank correlation between per capita aggregate transfers and per capita income is negative, implying thereby that he transfer of financial resources from the second to Eighth Finance Commission have been progressive with respect to per capita income of the States. (Per capita income is often considered as a proxy variable of economic development). But the degree of progressiveness has remained static over the years. The coefficient of rank correlation with per capita income hovers around –(0.7). A static progressiveness, has been inadequate to effectuate any reduction in the persisting inter-State disparities.
- Orissa has the first rank in the aggregate transfer of financial resources from Second to Eighth Finance Commission, but its thirteenth rank in per capita income in 1960-61, only improved marginally by one rank in 1990-91. This clearly implies that the financial resources transferred to Orissa, though were the highest, yet were not able to improve its position. Thus, the degree of progressiveness by the Finance Commission in the allocation of inter-State resources is inadequate. Hence, inter-State disparities persist till date, in spite of the huge quantum of federal transfers from the Union Government to the State Governments, through the allocation by Finance Commissions.
- Orissa was the only backward State which improved its ranking in per capita income terms (marginally) Bihar remained State at the last rank. Madhya Pradesh, Rajasthan and Uttar Pradesh declined in their per capita income status. This clearly implies, that the criteria adopted by the Finance Commissions in the devolution of tax-shares and awards of grants-in-aid require more progressiveness, if they are to reduce inter-State disparities. Three important criteria of devolution of

shareable proceeds of income tax and Union excise duties were population, contribution and a combination of the few indicators of backwardness. Population is neutral, contribution is regressive in nature and backwardness does not have adequate weightage. The net outcome is inadequate degree of progressiveness in the transfer of financial resources to the States.

TABLE 9

Ranking of States on the Basis of Per Capita Aggregate Federal Transfers and Per Capita Income

States	Per capita aggregate transfers 1957-58 to 1988-89	Per capita income 1970-71	Per capita income 1980-81	Per capita income 1990-91	Per capita income 1996-97
1	2	3	4	5	6
Gujarat	11	4	4	4	4
Haryana	14	2	2	3	3
Maharashtra	12	3	3	2	2
Punjab	13	1	1	1	1
Tamil Nadu	8	6	8	8	5
West Bengal	2	5	6	5	9
Andhra Pradesh	5	9	5	6	8
Karnataka	10	7	7	7	6
Kerala	3	8	9	10	7
Bihar	4	14	14	14	14
Madhya Pradesh	6	12.5	13	11	11
Orissa	1	12.5	11	12	13
Rajasthan	9	10	10	9	10
Uttar Pradesh	7	11	12	13	12

Source :

I. Col. (2) has been computed from Appendix 5.

II. Col. 3 to 6 have been computed from Col. 2 of tables 11 to 14.

Coefficient of rank correlation of per capita aggregate with per capita income :

1970-71 (-) 0.7
1980-81 (-) 0.7
1990-91 (-) 0.68
1996-97 (-) 0.77

After tax devolution some States may still have deficits in their revenue budgets. These are termed as post-devolution gaps in the non-plan revenue accounts of the States. The Constitution makers had realized that sharing of income-tax and Union excise duties might not be adequate to cover the needs of the States. Therefore, Article 275 provided for grants-in-aid to such States which parliament may determine are in need of assistance. This clearly shows that estimate of the need-revenue gap of the States is essential for determining the grants-in-aid to the States.

The objective of grants-in-aid to the States is to reduce the disparity among States on revenue account. With the passage of time the States should be able to overcome these inherent fiscal disadvantages. Grants-in-aid were to have a supplementary role in equating the fiscal capacities of the States. This has been clearly brought out by Ramanand Thakur.

The grants-in-aid overcome State financial disequilibrium resulting from the constitutional arrangement and also help in correcting inter-State disequilibrium which results from heterogeneity.

The important question is that how far were grants-in-aid able to equalize fiscal ranking of the States. Over the years the ranking of the States in accordance with their relative fiscal capacities in 1970-71, 1980-81, 1990-91 and 1996-97 computed in table 10 brings out the fact that Punjab State has the first rank in all the years, and the last rank is of Orissa in 1970-71, Rajasthan in 1980-81, Bihar in 1990-91 and again Orissa in 1996-97.

On the basis of table 10 States can be grouped by their performance in relative taxable capacity in 1996-97 as compared to 1970-71.

TABLE 10

Ranking of States in Accordance with Relative Taxable Capacity of States

States	Ranks according to relative taxable capacity 1970-71	Ranks according to relative taxable capacity 1980-81	Ranks according to relative taxable capacity 1990-91	Ranks according to relative taxable capacity 1996-97
1	2	3	4	5
Gujarat	3	4	5	3
Haryana	2	2	2	4
Maharashtra	4	3	3	2
Punjab	1	1	1	1
Tamil Nadu	5	11	8	7
West Bengal	6	5	6	6
Andhra Pradesh	9	7	4	5
Karnataka	8	8	7	8
Kerala	11	6	12	9.5
Bihar	13	13	14	13
Madhya Pradesh	12	10	9	11
Orissa	14	12	11	14
Rajasthan	7	14	10	9.5
Uttar Pradesh	10	9	13	12

Source : Computed from Col (9) of Tables 5-8 for the respective years.

Coefficient of rank correction between per capita income and relative taxable capacity of the respective years :

1970-71	(+) 0.4
1980-81	(+) 0.87
1990-91	(+) 0.95
1996-97	(+) 0.92

The States having improved performance in relative taxable capacity (RTC Rank 1996-97> RTC Rank 1970-71)	Maharashtra, Andhra Pradesh, Kerala, Madhya Pradesh.
The States having declined in relative taxable capacity (RTC Rank 1996-97<RTC Rank 1970-71)	Haryana, Tamil Nadu, Rajasthan, Uttar Pradesh.
The States having maintained relative taxable capacity (RTC Rank 1996-97 = RTC Rank 1970-71)	Gujarat, Punjab, Karnataka, West Bengal, Bihar, Orissa.

For reduction in inter-State disparities, the transfer of financial resources from the Finance Commissions should have improved the performance of backward States. Relative taxable capacity is nothing else but percentage of absolute taxable capacity to the Net State Domestic Product. The general viewpoint is that with the economic development of an economy, the absolute taxable capacity would increase, thereby, enlarging the base of States' own resources and relative taxable capacity would also increase.

The coefficient of rank correlation between per capita income and relative taxable capacity of the respective years 1970-71, 1980-81, 1990-91 and 1996-97 is positive and has increased from mere +0.4 in 1970-71 as reflected in Table 10 to as high as 0.96 in 1990-1991 and +0.92 in 1996-97. This clearly brings out the direct relationship between relative taxable capacity and per capita income.

Then one fails to understand, why Gujarat, Punjab and West Bengal, in spite of being advanced States failed to improve their relative taxable capacity over a period of four decades. Haryana and Tamil Nadu, another two advanced States had declined in relative taxable capacity performance over the years. The backward States except Madhya Pradesh either remained static or reflected a decline in relative taxable capacity.

The conclusion is obvious that backward States have been able to overcome their inherent fiscal disadvantages, in spite of the massive progressive financial resource transfers from the Finance Commission. Such a situation after four decades of transfer of resources by the Finance Commissions cannot be lauded. It needs immediate attention and restructuring.

But before deciding on the pattern of restructuring, the tax efforts of the States in accordance with their relative taxable capacity must be viewed. 'Equity with incentive' should form the basis of federal fiscal transfers. Inefficiency of States in raising resources must not be subsidized at any cost. Wastage of scarce financial resources is a luxury which we can ill-afford.

States must fulfil their tax obligations according to their relative taxable capacity. Tables 11-14 bring out the tax efforts of the States in mopping up their taxable capacity in relation to other States.

TABLE 11

Capacity Relatives and Effort Relatives of States (1970-71)

States	Per capita aggregate transfers 1957-58 to 1988-89	Per capita income 1970-71	Per capita income 1980-81	Per capita income 1990-91	Per capita income 1996-97
1	2	3	4	5	6
Gujarat	827	115	55	6.6	103
Haryana	960	134	56	5.8	91
Maharashtra	838	117	67	8.0	125
Punjab	1244	173	77	6.2	97
Tamil Nadu	669	93	50	7.5	117
West Bengal	781	109	43	5.5	86
Andhra Pradesh	627	87	44	7.0	109
Karnataka	664	92	48	7.2	112
Kerala	662	92	46	6.9	108
Bihar	415	58	29	7.0	109
Madhya Pradesh	575	80	34	5.9	92
Orissa	575	80	29	5.0	78
Rajasthan	618	86	37	6.0	94
Uttar Pradesh	603	84	32	5.3	83
Average index	718=100			6.4=100	

Source :

Col (4) : GOI, *Reserve Bank of India*, Bulletin, Bombay, Sept. 1972.

TABLE 12

Capacity Relatives and Effort Relatives of States (1980-81)

States	Per capita aggregate transfers 1957-58 to 1980-81	Capacity relative	Per capita tax (Rs.)	Tax effort (Per cent)	Effort Relative
1	2	3	4	5	6
Gujarat	2238	127	158	7	109
Haryana	2601	147	184	7	109
Maharashtra	2466	140	182	7.4	116
Punjab	3169	180	211	6.7	105
Tamil Nadu	1541	87	133	8.6	134
West Bengal	1645	93	97	5.9	92
Andhra Pradesh	1659	94	110	6.6	103
Karnataka	1644	93	130	7.9	123
Kerala	1445	82	133	9.2	144
Bihar	1007	57	40	4	62
Madhya Pradesh	1240	70	73	5.9	92
Orissa	1308	74	51	3.9	61
Rajasthan	1429	81	68	4.8	75
Utar Pradesh	1296	73	59	4.6	72
Average Index	1763=100			6.4=100	

Source :

Col. (4) Reserve Bank of India, Bombay, *Report on Currency and Finance*, 1980-81, Vol. 11, p. 116.

TABLE 13

Capacity Relatives and Effort Relatives of States (1970-71)

States	Per capita income 1990-91	Per capita relative	Per capita tax (Rs.)	Tax effort per cent	Effort Relative
1	2	3	4	5	6
Gujarat	5850	117	471	8.0	100
Haryana	7516	150	522	6.9	86
Maharashtra	7598	152	549	7.8	87
Punjab	8423	168	551	6.5	81
Tamil Nadu	4619	92	479	10	125
West Bengal	4794	96	359	7.5	94
Andhra Pradesh	4731	94	420	8.9	111
Karnataka	4631	92	443	9.6	120
Kerala	4032	80	451	11	137
Bihar	2650	53	231	8.7	109
Madhya Pradesh	4021	80	318	7.9	99
Orissa	3596	72	272	7.6	95
Rajasthan	4035	81	294	7.3	91
Utar Pradesh	3557	71	271	7.6	95
Average Index	5004=100			8.0=100	

Source :

Col. (4) Bagchi Amaresh and Tapas Sen, *Budgetary Trends and Plan Financing in the States*, table 2.15, p.90.

TABLE 14

Capacity Relatives and Effort Relatives of States (1996-97)

States	Per capita income 1990-91	Per capita relative	Per capita tax (Rs.)	Tax effort per cent	Effort Relative
1	2	3	4	5	6
Gujarat	14875	136	1332	9.6	120
Haryana	16392	150	1155	7.1	89
Maharashtra	17666	162	1353	7.8	97
Punjab	18008	165	1223	6.7	84
Tamil Nadu	11708	107	1343	11.5	144
West Bengal	9579	88	571	6.0	75
Andhra Pradesh	10308	94	676	6.8	85
Karnataka	10504	96	1169	11.4	142
Kerala	10309	94	1260	13.9	174
Bihar	4231	39	242	6.3	79
Madhya Pradesh	7571	69	553	7.4	92
Orissa	5893	54	390	6.1	76
Rajasthan	8974	82	628	7.4	92
Uttar Pradesh	6713	61	402	6.0	75
Average index	10909=100			8=100	

Source :

Col. (4) has been worked out from the Total Tax Revenue figures given in the *Reserve Bank of India Bulletin*, Feb. 1999 and the population figures of Col (4) and Col (8) of table 4.

The term capacity relative of the States is the average index of States per capita income estimated in col (2) and the term effort relative is the average index of the percentage of per capita tax of a State to its per capita income, computed in col (6). The grouping of the States on the basis of capacity relative and effort relative is as follows :

	1970-71	1980-81	1990-91	1996-97
States having effort relative greater then their capacity relative (ER>CR)	Maharashtra, Tamil Nadu, Andhra Pradesh, Karnataka, Kerala, Bihar, Rajasthan	Tamil Nadu, Andhra Pradesh, Karnataka, Kerala, Bihar, Madhya Pradesh	Tamil Nadu, Andhra Pradesh, Karnataka, Kerala, Bihar, Madhya Pradesh, Orissa, Rajasthan, Uttar Pradesh	Tamil Nadu, Karnataka, Kerala, Bihar, Madhya Pradesh, Orissa, Rajasthan, Uttar Pradesh
States having effort relative lower than their capacity relative (ER<CR)	Gujarat, Haryana, Punjab, West Bengal, Orissa, Uttar Pradesh	Gujarat, Haryana, Maharashtra, Punjab, West Bengal, Orissa, Rajasthan, Uttar Pradesh	Gujarat, Haryana, Maharashtra, Punjab, West Bengal, Orissa, Rajasthan, Uttar Pradesh	Gujarat, Haryana, Maharashtra, Punjab, West Bengal, Orissa, Rajasthan, Uttar Pradesh
States having effort relative equal to their capacity relative (ER=CR)	Madhya Pradesh	-	-	-

Except for Tamil Nadu and Maharashtra in 1970-71, no other advanced State had effort relative greater than their capacity relative. Tamil Nadu has maintained this status till 1996-97. But Maharashtra has been having effort relative lower than capacity effort since 1980-81. The other advanced States Punjab, Haryana, Gujarat and West Bengal have effort relative lower than their capacity relative since 1970-71, whereas, Bihar needing aid desperately has effort relative greater than its capacity relative since 1970-71. This is a State which emerged as a positive absolute taxable capacity State only recently in 1996-97. Rajasthan, Madhya Pradesh, Orissa and Uttar Pradesh have also, effort relative greater than their capacity relative since 1990-91. Backward States collecting own resources more than what is warranted by their capacity is highly appreciable. At the same time advanced States must be penalized for not collecting taxes according to what their capacity warrants.

Economic backwardness is a self-feeding process. A backward State in a backward country has a double disability. The economic backwardness of the country and that of the State interact and reinforce one another. A large proportion of population in these

States live under conditions that are unsatisfactory as compared to those prevailing elsewhere in India.

Conditions which can be defined sub-human in absolute terms. Everyone living anywhere in India is entitled to equity in respect of development of facilities like roads, electrification, health and education by the very fact of being a citizen of this democracy. Their development is a matter of national commitment. The traditional 'trickle down' theory of development has failed to automatically solve the problem of backward States.

Ever since independence, the issue of inequalities in the level of development of various States has agitated economists, politicians and of course the people of the backward States. It becomes obvious to anyone travelling by a bus or train from west to East, or North to South that India remains a land of contrasts. As one starts from Amritsar on a journey to Calcutta one notices how the people of Punjab are much healthier, better dressed and obviously wealthier than those of Uttar Pradesh and Bihar. Similarly travelling from Delhi to Bombay or to Gujarat one realizes how with a change of landscape and State boundaries one comes across miles and miles of sand-dunes and 'wilting' crops in Rajasthan, uneven terrain in Madhya Pradesh with narrow roads winding through forests, pock marked mining towns, tribals huddled together on railway platforms and bus stands and jawar-bazra and oilseed crops struggling to survive without irrigation.

So far the Finance Commissions have given grants-in-aid to States on the basis of budgetary deficits. The States find indirect (and unintended) encouragement, that no matter how poor their resource mobilization efforts are and how high their level of expenditure, the non-plan revenue gap would be made good by the Finance Commission. Had Punjab made efforts at revenue collection, at least equal to what it fiscal capacity warranted, it would not be in its present financial plight. There is no reason why the highest per capita income State, since four decades should hold a begging bowl before the Union Government. This will be highly undesirable situation anywhere, and the results can be disastrous. Resources are grossly inadequate and urgently required to supplement the low fiscal base of the backward States. Backward States have made efforts at revenue collection more than what their capacity warranted. They must be given incentives.

'Equity with incentive' should form the basis of restructuring federal fiscal transfer. Inefficiency of States in raising resources must not be subsidized at any cost. Wastage of scarce financial resources is a luxury which we can ill-afford. So far federal transfers, in spite of being progressive, have not been able to make any dent on inter-State disparities, even though the backward States, by and large have not been found lacking in self-help.

A State may be poor or rich, backward or advanced, underdeveloped or developed, in absolute terms, but its backwardness is relative to other State's development. This inter-State disparities can be reduced only when federal transfers are in accordance with the relative fiscal capacity of the States.

NOTES AND REFERENCES

1. *Note 1* : Explanation of the computation of tables (1-4).
2. Nurkse, R. : *Problems of Capital Formation in Under-developed Countries*, Oxford University Press, 1973, Delhi.
3. Appendix 2 : Incremental capital output ratio on an average is 3.70 and growth rate of Net National Domestic Product on an average is 4.0.

   Appendix 3 : Annual rate of population growth is 2.2 per cent, on an average from 1951-91.

   Appendix 4 : Percentage of private and public investment during the five year plans, reflects that on an average private investment is about 45 of the total from First Five Year Plan to Seventh Five Year Plan.
4. Thakur Ramanand : *Finance Commission and Centre-State Relations in India*, Deep and Deep Publications, New Delhi, 1982, p. 126.

NOTE I

Steps involved in computation of tables 1-4 relating to essential consumption.

Step 1 : Appendix I per capita, per month and annual essential consumption is estimated at State specific poverty line in 1973-74, separately for rural and urban population at 1960-61 prices.

Step 2 : Table 1 per capita and total essential consumption of rural, urban and total essential consumption is estimated for 1970-71.

Col (3) is estimate of per capita annual essential consumption in monetary terms of rural population at 1970-71 State-specific prices. For example for Gujarat :

$$\text{PCAEC} = \frac{562}{248} \times 73 = \text{Rs. } 392$$

i.e.,

$$\frac{\text{PCAEC(rural)}1973-74}{\text{Prices(rural)}1973-74} \times \text{Prices(rural)}1970-71$$

Source : $\frac{\text{Appendix 1 (col4)}}{\text{Appendix 1 (col2)}} \times \text{table (col. 2)}$

Col. (5) is an estimate of total annual essential consumption of rural population of the State obtained by the product of col (3) and col .(4).

Col. (7) and col (9) relate to urban population of the State and its total annual essential consumption computed in a similar manner.

Col (10) is the total essential consumption of the State obtained by the summation of col (5) and col (9).

Tables 2, 3 and 4 reflect the total essential consumption of the States for the years 1980-81, 1990-91 and 1996-97 respectively.

Since for the entire population of a State actual consumption is assumed to be equal to essential consumption, therefore, the surplus that would emerge from the population whose actual consumption is less than essential consumption is not treated as a part of fiscal capacity available to a State for resource mobilization. (it is not a part of non-invested surplus).

Appendix I

Per Capita, Per Months and Annual Essential Consumption in 1973-74 at 1960-61=100 (base) (1970-71)

States	Price Index 1973-74 Rural	PCPM EC 1973 -74 Rural (Rs.)	PCAEC 1973-74 Rural (Rs.)	Prices index 1973-74 Urban	PCPMEC 1973-74 Urban (Rs.)	PCAEC 1973-74 Urban (Rs.)
1	2	3	4	5	6	7
Gujarat	248.56	47.10	562.20	246.01	60.08	721
Haryana	282.23	49.95	599.40	255.54	52.07	625
Maharashtra	283.01	50.47	605.60	240.34	58.64	704
Punjab	282.23	49.95	599.40	254.22	51.80	622
Tamil Nadu	246.57	45.09	541.10	239.96	54.34	652
West Bengal	277.92	54.49	653.90	242.71	54.69	656
Andhra Pradesh	244.54	41.71	500.50	250.50	55.11	661
Karnataka	283.46	47.24	566.90	266.53	57.87	694
Kerala	286.85	51.68	620.20	273.03	62.08	745
Bihar	334.55	57.68	692.20	273.23	60.29	723
Madhya Pradesh	316.62	50.20	603.40	276.48	63.65	764
Orissa	283.27	46.87	562.40	245.97	60.18	722
Rajasthan	291.86	50.96	611.50	268.64	60.77	729
Uttar Pradesh	306.93	48.92	587.00	270.80	56.81	682

Source : Government of India : *Report of the Expert Group on Estimation of Proportion and Number of Poor* : Perspective Planning Division, Planning Commission, New Delhi, July 1993.

Col. (2) and (3) : Consumer Price Index for Agricultural Labour.

Col. (5) and (6) : Consumer Price Index Number of Industrial Workers.

APPENDIX 2

	Incremental capital output ratio	Growth rate of Net National Domestic Product
1	2	3
First Five Year Plan	2.87	3.5
Second Five Year Plan	3.56	4.0
Third Five Year Plan	6.13	2.6
Fourth Five Year Plan	4.79	3.2
Fifth Five Year Plan	3.36	4.8
Seventh Five Year Plan	2.72	5.6
Sixth Five Year Plan	2.74	5.5
Average	3.70	4.0

Source : Prasad K.N., *Indian Economy Since* 1951 : *Growth with Imbalances*, Intellectual Publishing House, New Delhi, 1993, pp. 409 and 411.

Note : Incremental Capital Output Ratio :

Eighth Five Year Plan	4.24
Ninth Five Year Plan	4.08
Post Ninth Five Year Plan	4.05

Source : Government of India, Planning Commission, *Approach Paper to the Ninth Five Year Plan* 1997-2002, p. 32.

APPENDIX 3

Annual Rate of Population Growth

Year	Percentage
1	2
1951-61	2.0
1961-71	2.2
1971-81	2.2
1981-91	2.1
1951-91	2.2

Source : Centre for Monitoring Indian Economy, Basic Statistics : States, *Monthly Review of the Indian Economy*, Economic Intelligence Services, Bombay, September 1994, table 1.1.

APPENDIX 4

Percentage of Private and Public Investment during the Five Year Plans

	Private investment	Public investment
1	2	3
First Five Year Plan	53.6	46.4
Second Five Year Plan	45.4	54.6
Third Five Year Plan	36.3	63.7
Fourth Five Year Plan	39.7	60.3
Fifth Five Year Plan	42.4	57.6
Seventh Five Year Plan	47.1	52.9
Sixth Five Year Plan	52.2	47.8
Average	45.0	54.7

Source : Prasad, K.N. : *Indian Economy Since* 1951 : Growth with Imbalances, Intellectual Publishing House, 1993, p. 88.

APPENDIX 5

Per Capita Transfers recommended from the Second Finance Commission to the Eighth Finance Commission

(Rs.)

States	Second Finance Comm.	Third Finance Comm.	Fourth Finance Comm.	Fifth Finance Comm-ission	Sixth Finance Comm-ission	Seventh Finance Comm-ission	Eighth Finance Comm-ission	Aggregate per capita transfer
1	2	3	4	5	6	7	8	9
Gujarat	18.52	38.70	29.82	86.45	122.07	282.66	436.67	952.23
Haryana	—	—	22.34	75.27	105.84	239.20	640.48	747.67
Maharashtra	29.26	28.39	33.60	96.59	126.61	272.94	419.65	944.97
Punjab	29.83	29.23	28.64	83.21	111.90	249.72	384.61	891.37
Tamil Nadu	22.31	26.27	33.39	90.00	120.76	310.66	509.28	1067.69
West Bengal	21.84	24.95	28.58	101.34	167.26	292.51	631.86	1215.08
Andhra Pradesh	25.92	32.23	34.58	94.89	161.00	284.58	541.41	1114.11
Karnataka	32.83	32.40	47.56	84.40	115.25	270.89	465.76	983.60
Kerala	23.51	38.07	57.33	109.29	206.00	302.09	505.20	1173.09
Bihar	21.56	20.73	22.19	90.20	134.51	316.58	603.79	1159.56
Madhya Pradesh	23.68	25.29	25.79	82.28	116.42	306.03	506.61	1091.56
Orissa	28.55	54.20	68.54	131.22	239.55	372.00	723.35	1533.13
Rajasthan	25.49	32.32	32.34	102.73	189.23	263.21	488.68	1051.04
Uttar Pradesh	19.86	19.01	25.56	87.48	136.27	298.89	550.50	1087.21

Source : Sastry M.L. and G.R. Reddy : Centre-State Financial Relations, Centre for Economic and Social Studies, Hyderabad, Concept Publishing Company, New Delhi, 1988, p. 144.

13

EMERGING ISSUES IN THE MANAGEMENT OF FISCAL DEFICIT

—J.R. Gupta

There is no doubt that the finances of the various State Government, or for that matter, even those of the Union Government are in the mess. Periodically the State Governments have to delay the payment of even salaries, pensions, and other committed expenditure of routine nature, *i.e.,* expenditure on current account. Now this system of managing public finances is not sustainable. Already this has led to explosive situation the like we witnessed in 1991, when India had not only to pledge gold to tide over the economic crisis but also had to unwittingly yield to external pressure. Therefore, in order to maintain our self-esteem high it is essential to maintain our financial house in order.

Now the question arises, what are the genesis of the problem and what is the way out? It is a well known fact that the revenue of the Government, particularly current account revenue or revenue account receipts have fallen short of current account expenditure or expenditure on revenue account.* Then on revenue account, burgeoning non-plan expenditure is the main culprit so much so that the Government is compelled to use borrowings or even plan expenditure to pay salaries or pensions. It is estimated that to implement the plan schemes in many

States the contributions from their own sources are negative. Now salaries, interest payments and subsidies are the three important components of non-plan expenditure on revenue account.

* As per Eleventh Finance Commission (XI FC) revenue deficit constitutes nearly 2/3rd of the fiscal deficit.

While salaries and pensions account for as high as 60-70 per cent of total expenditure, interest payments and debt servicing account for nearly 25-30 per cent. Therefore, nothing is left for plan and developmental purposes. That is why whenever we hear about curtailing expenditure to reduce deficit, the axe has to fall on subsidies. Although, the issue of subsidies needs a full debate which is outside the scope of this paper yet some basics about the use of subsidies should be kept in mind. Since subsidies have some social and economic costs, therefore, while granting subsides care should be taken that these serve some social and economic objectives. If socio-economic benefits outweigh socio-economic costs, only then the subsidies are justified. Take the case of agricultural subsidies. If these subsidies add to total agricultural production, or induce the desirable shifts in cropping pattern, or lead to more equitable distribution of income, or fulfill any other socio-economic objectives, then these are justified. Otherwise these subsidies would be harming the farmers themselves more than any other sector of the economy. Because then the State Governments would be starved of funds and hence they have to cut investment expenditure or developmental expenditure.

Now from here where we should go. From the view point of management of resources and to come out of this mess, we have to adopt both short term and long term, and even medium term measures. First, let us study the pattern of revenue of the State Governments, which reveals that nearly 40-50 per cent of State tax revenue comes from sales tax, followed by State excise duty (25-30 per cent). Land revenue and entertainment taxes have become losing sources of revenue. Percentage share of stamps and registration fee and even taxes on passengers and goods is on the decline. Revenue from MVT (motor vehicles tax) is another minor but growing source of tax revenue.

Again, it is very interesting to find that in some States while total consumption of the State is increasing, sales tax revenue is falling. Though this may be due to tax evasion on the part of the trading communities, yet as a student of economics one can say that the consumption pattern in the society has changed and our tax structure does not reflect the same. For example, we are now spending more on petrol and petroleum products, electricity and electric gadgets, communication services like telephone, fax, pager, mobile phones, etc. and so on. Then new sources of entertainment have come up with the result that old entertainment tax has become outmoded. Services have emerged as a fast growing sector of the economy and now constitutes nearly 50 per cent of the GDP and "it is imperative to increasingly bring in services under the tax net for improving the buoyancy of indirect taxes."* To bring the services under tax net value added tax is the best alternative. In modern days when sale prices of durable commodities like refrigerators, air-conditioners, micro-waves, washing machines, etc. include service charges, warranty charges, installation charges, etc. the value added component would obviously be more than the original price. In such circumstances the States can collect more tax revenue through the levy of value added tax or till it is not possible due to constitutional hindrances, the States should go for the final stage sales tax. The point which has to be emphasized is that the Government must make efforts to impose new taxes which reflect the changing life style of the people *i.e.,* taxes should be imposed on gods or services having higher income elasticity. Taxes on nursing homes, hotels, restaurants, advertisements, motor vehicles, petrol, new sources of entertainment, vacant residential plots, etc. are some such examples. Then across the board 5-10 per cent increase in user charges, including bus fare can be imposed. The recent hike in bus fare in Punjab State by about 8-10 per cent has gone unnoticed. To achieve the canon of expediency, which is essential in a democracy it must be mentioned here that the additional tax and non-tax burden should be administered in marginal doses so as to check the resistance of the tax payers. But once it is levied, there should be no rolling back. When the Government retraces its steps it loses its credibility and tax payers suffer, while middlemen galore.

But let us admit one thing very clearly that there is not much scope of raising revenue from taxes by increasing the rates of existing taxes. What is required is to widen the tax net by

* GOI, Ministry of Finance, Report of the Eleventh Financae Commission, Aklank Publications, New Delhi, p. 27.

incorporating such new taxes as they reflect the changing life pattern of the people. In a recent workshop on "Rejuvination of Punjab's Economy with Special Reference to Fiscal Problems" organised by Punjabi University (December, 1999), it was emphasised that :

Now commodities and services be identified which concern improvements in social sector and quality of life be slowly brought under the tax-net. For example, every shopkeeper with telephone must be made to have sales tax number and a minimum slot of tax be imposed on him/her in the initial phase, on the pattern of presumptive tax introduced by Central Board of Direct Taxes.

Still more important is the tax enforcement. Tax payers should be educated and encouraged to pay taxes honestly. Tax arrears should be realised and tax evaders should not be protected under any circumstances by the political bosses. In this regard, the Eleventh Finance Commission has observed that "Massive arrears of assessed but uncollected revenues remain on the account books of both Central and State governments. Effective steps for collecting these arrears in the next few years can help to ease the resources position of governments at both levels."*

However, it may be reiterated that already the share of tax revenue in many States has risen from 40-50 per cent in 1967-68 to 65-70 per cent in 2000. Consequently the share of non-tax revenue has fallen. And in the event of liberatlisation, privatisation and globalisation many taxes will have to be removed. For example, our super-fine variety of rice is not competitive in international markets because of heavy taxes like purchase tax, market fee, rural development charges, etc. So, therefore, the State Governments will have to shed off many levies to make their products internationally competitive. The point which has to emphasised is that non-tax sources have to be tapped afresh. The major sources of non-tax revenue are General Services, Economic Services, Social and Community Services, Interest and Dividends. Now leaving aside interest and dividends, which form a separate category. We can divide the non-tax source's services into merit services and non-merit services, and

* *Ibid.*, p. 28.

even in between the two. While education, medical services and safe drinking water come into the merit category, issuing and the renewal of driving licenses, transport services, etc., can constitute non-merit services. There should be no two opinions that non-merit services should be charged at market and even at higher prices. The old rates have become outmoded. For example, one has to pay a fee of only Rs. 15/- for the renewal of driving license, Rs. 30/- for the issue of learner's license, etc. And these fees can easily be increased by three to four times. Even in respect of merit goods or services a marginal increase in rates is possible. A moderate increase of about 10 per cent in the user charges if the existing charges are high and 50-100 per cent if existing charges are very low is likely to go unnoticed. The point which has to be emphasised is that in the short-run Government has to mobilise revenue from every conceivable source, and for this item-by-item detailed exercise has to be carried out by each and every Government department.

Simultaneously efforts will have to be made to prune and rationalize public expenditure. As already stated expenditure on salaries and pensions constitute a bulk of the total current expenditure. Wherever possible the Government should try to introduce zero-based budgeting *i.e.,* the Government must prepare every year budget afresh and justify the expenditure on each and every item. If warranted by zero-based budgeting, departments serving the same objectives must be merged. Any additional expenditure must be thoroughly examined in terms of cost-benefit analysis. Budgetary support to the public sector undertakings (PSUs) must be justified on the ground of maximising social welfare. Otherwise PSUs may be made autonomous and told to finance at least their current account expenditure. Efforts will have to be made to move towards zero revenue deficit. In fact the main culprit of fiscal deficit has been the galloping revenue deficit. Already the ratio of revenue deficit of fiscal deficit had increased to 67.52 per cent in case of the Centre and to 56.86 per cent in case of the States.* Therefore, fiscal deficit would automatically be pruned if revenue deficit is tapered off. To put a cap on public

* *Ibid.*, pp. 177-78.

borrowings the Centre has already decided to enact the Fiscal Responsibility and Budget Management Bill. But simultaneously efforts should be made to use the proceeds from disinvestment of PSUs for redeeming the public debt or for building socio-economic infrastructure so as to meet the cherished goals of equity and removal of poverty. Under no circumstances proceeds from disinvestment be used for consumption purposes *i.e.,* current account expenditure.

In the long run it is being realized that until and unless the local self governments *viz.*, Panchayats and Municipalities are given some financial autonomy much is not possible. In fact now there is an opportunity for the State Governments to involve these institutions in the mobilisation of resources and pass on to them some of the financial burden. Collection of land revenue and entertainment tax, two major losing sources of revenue can be entrusted to them. If Panchayats and urban local bodies are assured that the entire proceeds from these taxes would remain with them they might develop a keen interest in exploiting these and other sources. Then motor vehicles tax (tractors in most of the States have been hitherto exempted from this tax) and tax on rents particularly on property rented out to the governments/semi-governments agencies or property put to commercial uses (like petrol pump) or any other form of property tax can be other productive sources of revenue. To make the local bodies self-reliant, they can be given some share in State taxes, *viz.*, excise duty, fees on the registration of property, etc. The State Governments can also levy a surcharge on the existing taxes particularly for the benefits of Panchayats and Municipalities. In order to fight with agricultural calamities there is an urgent need to create a Relief Fund on the pattern of National Calamity Relief Fund. At the same time efforts should be intensified to start a comprehensive crop insurance policy. For this purpose insurance cess on the agricultural produce must be levied.

To conclude one can say that the main culprit of fiscal deficit has been the revenue deficit. Principle of sound public finance is that consumption expenditure; *i.e.,* expenditure on revenue account, must be financed by current income, *i.e.,* receipts on revenue account. Consumption expenditure financed through borrowings, or even by running down of assets, is unsustainable. However, one cannot set a precise limit for fiscal deficit or for deficit spending. Much depends upon the economic fundamentals. If foreign exchange position is comfortable and prices are reasonably stable, the Centre may finance its development expenditure through monetized deficit. However, the problem of imbalance in resources and expenditure is more serious in case of the States, where competitive populism among the political parties is playing havoc with State finances. But it must be borne in mind that it is the performance and governance on the development front which weigh more in the minds of the voters than the mere distribution of doles.

LIST OF CONTRIBUTORS

Bansal, R.K. (Dr.), Reader, Department of Economics, Punjabi University, Patiala (Punjab).

Bhargava, P.K., Professor and Head, Department of Economics Banaras Hindu University, Varanasi (U.P.).

Dhingra, Dhanpreet Singh, Programmer, Punjab School of Economics, Guru Nanak Dev University, Amritsar (Punjab).

Giri, C., Deputy Registrar, Indian Institute of Public Administration, New Delhi.

Gupta, J.R. (Dr.), Professor, Department of Economics, Punjabi University, Patiala (Punjab).

Jani, B.M. (Dr.), Professor, Department of Economics, Saurashtra University, Rajkot (Gujarat).

Jena, Pratap Ranjan (Dr.), Economist, National Institute of Public Finance and Policy, New Delhi.

Kalra, Manjit (Dr.), Head, Department of Economics, Government College for Girls, Sector 11, Chandigarh.

Murty, S. (Dr.), Professor and Head, Department of Economics Vikram University, Ujjain (M.P.).

Parkash, Om (Dr.), Professor, Punjab School of Economics, Guru Nanak Dev University, Amritsar, (Punjab).

Raikhy Navjot, Lecturer, Post graduate Department of Economics, D.A.V. College, Amritsar (Punjab).

Reddy, Y.V. (Dr.), Deputy Governor, Reserve Bank of India, Mumbai (Maharashtra).

Satyanarayan, B. (Dr.), Professor of Economics, Osmania University, Hyderabad (Andhra Pradesh).

Sharma, Chandra Ballabh (Dr.), Reader, Department of Economics Kurukshetra University, Kurukshetra (Haryana).

Sooden, Meenakshi (Dr.), Department of Economics, Himachal Pradesh University, Shimla (H.P.).